SIT

SIT

Twenty-Eight Days to a Rock-Solid Daily Meditation Habit

Bodhipaksa

Wisdom Publications
132 Perry Street
New York, NY 10014 USA
wisdom.org

Library of Congress Cataloging-in-Publication Data is available.
Names: Bodhipaksa, 1961– author
Title: SIT: twenty-eight days to a rock-solid daily meditation habit / Bodhipaksa.
Description: First edition. | New York: Wisdom Publications, 2026. |
Includes index.
Identifiers: LCCN 2025026042 (print) | LCCN 2025026043 (ebook) |
ISBN 9798890700087 paperback | ISBN 9798890700179 ebook
Subjects: LCSH: Meditation—Buddhism | Śamatha (Buddhism) |
Spiritual life—Buddhism
Classification: LCC BQ5612 .B628 2026 (print) | LCC BQ5612 (ebook) |
DDC 294.3/4435—dc23/eng/20250918
LC record available at https://lccn.loc.gov/2025026042
LC ebook record available at https://lccn.loc.gov/2025026043

ISBN 979-8-89070-008-7 ebook ISBN 979-8-89070-017-9

30 29 28 27 26
5 4 3 2 1

Cover art and design by Marc Whitaker. Interior design by Tim Holtz.

Printed on acid-free paper that meets the guidelines for permanence and durability of the Production Guidelines for Book Longevity of the Council on Library Resources.

Printed in the United States of America.

Contents

Introduction

Don't you admire those people who can meditate year after year without ever missing a day? I always have. But for a long time I was envious of them as well, because I was unable to sustain that kind of regularity. Sure, there had always been stretches when I'd sit daily without fail—sometimes for months at a time—but inevitably I'd start missing days, and sometimes a week would go by where I'd sat only once or twice. Yes, I knew meditation was important, but it seemed like a luxury I couldn't afford in my time-poor life. After a retreat, my practice would become regular for a while, but the momentum would fizzle out and I'd be back to sitting erratically. Each New Year offered a fresh start, but it was always the same dynamic: a run of success that ultimately faltered. It was a mystery to me how some people managed to maintain what I now call a Rock-Solid Daily Meditation Practice.

I tried to convince myself that this irregularity didn't matter. After all, even though my practice was erratic, it was helping me. It calmed me. It helped me be kinder. I'd even had some particularly deep meditations among all the busyness. But my meditation practice being irregular bothered me. No matter how hard I tried, no matter how many times I recommitted myself to daily practice, I just couldn't stick to it. The worst part was that as a meditation teacher I felt hypocritical encouraging others to meditate regularly when I was struggling to do so myself. I couldn't sugarcoat the fact that I was failing at something that ought to be basic.

A lot of irregular meditators experience this sense of failure. You're just not the kind of person who can meditate daily. You lack the willpower that other meditators have, and you'll never have it. This is the kind of story we tell ourselves. This narrative is meant to explain why we haven't been able to establish a daily practice, but it ends up becoming a self-fulfilling prophecy, telling us that we never will be a Rock-Solid Daily Meditator. Our "failure" narrative gives us permission to give up trying.

Asking people how they sustain a daily practice long term is rarely enlightening. If someone's naturally good at something and has never had to strive at it, they often can't explain their secret. I remember when a woman I was dating took me ice skating for the first time. She could glide over the ice, making tight turns and spins with a natural grace and elegance. When I wasn't clinging to the handrail I took hesitant, shaky steps, my feet slipping out from under me, my arms flailing to prevent me from crashing to the ice below. Her advice? "Don't wobble!" The thing is, I didn't know how not to wobble! When something comes easily to you, it can be hard to put yourself in the shoes of someone who struggles. It's hard to guide someone through a process you haven't been through yourself.

So I had to figure out from scratch how to become a Rock-Solid Daily Meditator. Not only did I learn to sit every day, but doing so was much easier than I thought it would be—or at least it was once I'd figured out strategies that supported my intention to sit daily. I even managed to achieve this at a particularly challenging time in my life, while I was busier and more stressed than I'd ever been. And this timing turned out to be perfect. Sitting daily helped me get through one of the most difficult times of my life.

Having worked out how to establish a daily practice for myself, I shared what I had learned with my meditation students. They found that it worked for them too. They discovered their own approaches, some of which helped me too. Their discoveries became part of my own practice and teaching, which went through further cycles of sharing, discussion, clarification, and refinement. What I bring to you in this book is an approach to meditating daily that was developed collectively. Together, my students and I evolved a collection of tools that has been helpful to many people. There are no guarantees, though. You, a meditator who wants to sit daily without fail, need to do some work in intelligently applying the principles outlined here. "You yourselves must strive. The Buddhas only point the way," as the Buddha himself said.[1] Not that I'm anywhere close to being a buddha, but you get the drift.

Since this book is about overcoming longstanding difficulties with establishing a daily meditation practice, I'm assuming that you've probably been meditating for a while. But if, for some reason, you're just setting out on your meditation journey, you're still welcome to proceed. I won't be offering you a step-by-step guide to meditating—that's outside the remit of this book—but the guided meditations that accompany this program will teach you the basics, and there are also some written pointers in Appendix 2. If you're just starting off, I hope you'll find that your meditation habit becomes firmly established from the get-go.

The Myth of Willpower

The main obstacle I had to overcome in establishing a regular daily practice was the belief that willpower is the key to establishing good habits. Who doesn't want to have willpower? It's been drummed into us that this is what we need if we want to achieve anything significant. But psychologists have shown that willpower plays no role whatsoever in developing and sustaining new habits. In one study, a six-week training course in self-control failed to help participants to change *any habits at all* in their lives. Even worse, participants found that trying to exercise self-control left them emotionally drained.[2] Exercising willpower doesn't work and makes you feel terrible. Some people will boast about their high levels of willpower—it's a highly prestigious thing to brag about having—but they're not necessarily describing what's really happening. Another study on willpower showed that those who believed they were good at resisting temptation were those who were least exposed to temptation in the first place.[3] They rated themselves highly on their willpower, yet they were not using willpower. What we *think* we're doing isn't necessarily what we *are* doing.

People who are good at overcoming bad habits, and so appear to have willpower, tend to avoid putting themselves into positions where they need to resist temptation. Rather than walk past the donut shop and end up battling with their cravings, they simply walk down a different street. They put the alarm clock on the other side of the room so that they aren't tempted to stay in bed. Some might think that these are examples of willpower, but they aren't: Willpower involves using the strength of your resolve so you can overcome temptation and attain a goal. Willpower is fighting yourself and winning. When you strategically keep temptations out of sight and out of mind, you may be making wise choices, but this isn't willpower. It's a different approach altogether: rather than fighting yourself and winning, you're strategically avoiding getting into fights with yourself. We can call this self-control or motivational strategizing, but it's misleading to call it willpower.

The famous "marshmallow study," done in 1970 by the Stanford psychologist Walter Mischel, was meant to be a test of willpower, but a closer look calls into question whether that's what was really going on. In this study, preschool children with an average age of four and a half were put in a room by themselves, sitting at a desk on which there was a marshmallow. They were told that if they could go fifteen minutes without eating the marshmallow, they would be given a second marshmallow. Getting two marshmallows instead of one is a huge deal when you're that age. But fifteen minutes alone in a room is a long time, especially with temptation right in front of you. As you'd expect, some kids earned the second marshmallow, but others succumbed to temptation.

We might assume that this study showed which kids had willpower and which lacked it. That's not really what happened. Willpower is about forcibly controlling your actions through the strength of your desire. But the kids who didn't eat the first marshmallow were successful not because of the strength of their desire. They were successful because they had strategies to help them direct their attention away from the marshmallow.

The strategies the kids used included singing songs, wriggling in their seats, covering their eyes, doing little dances, pretending that the marshmallow was something that they hated, looking everywhere but directly in front of them, and in every possible way avoiding the delicious temptation that was sitting right there on the desk. One kid even put herself to sleep. The more strategies children had, the longer they were able to resist temptation. Imagine that you're one of the kids who, for whatever reason, had never learned to do these kinds of things. What do you do? You stare at the marshmallow and say to yourself, "I must not eat the treat!" You try using willpower! But this means you're keeping your focus on the treat, and this in turn makes you more likely to eat it. If two children have an equally strong desire to attain a goal, the one who has the most effective strategies to get there is most likely to succeed.[4] The idea behind willpower is that if you make yourself want something strongly enough, it'll happen. But without strategies, no amount of wanting will work.

Now it might seem like I'm making a distinction so subtle that it amounts to pedantry, but it's actually important. If you want to meditate daily, success will not come from increasing the desire to meditate daily. If you've struggled with this for years, you already have all the desire you need. What you lack are strategies for reminding yourself to sit, for handling thoughts and feelings of resistance, for making it feel good to meditate, and for fitting the habit of sitting into an already busy schedule. When we focus on willpower instead of strategies, we're doing something that doesn't make a difference—and so we fail. We blame this failure on a "lack of willpower," telling ourselves that what we need is a stronger desire. And so we fail again. That's why we can go decades with an erratic meditation habit.

People for whom daily meditation practice comes naturally are those who have adopted, often unconsciously, strategies that support their intention. This is great news for anyone who has difficulty committing to sit, because if we are willing to learn those strategies then we too can become Rock-Solid Daily Meditators. Certainly, that's been my experience, and it's been the experience of hundreds of my meditation students. It's been exciting to watch people recording their progress: 28 days in a row, 100 days, 365 days, 1,000 days. I recently heard from two people who were on one of my early Get Your Sit Together courses, who had just recorded their 4,000th consecutive day of practice. That's 11 years of unbroken daily practice—not missing even one single day—which really is astonishing.[5]

So what we're going to do is to learn strategies that support daily practice. I'll suggest many of these. Generally we're like those preschoolers in the classroom—we need lots of tools at our disposal, because one strategy on its own might not be enough. So we need another, and maybe another, and another. These strategies work together to help us find success.

Before we get started on Day 1 I'd like to introduce you to one particularly important strategy that we'll employ throughout this program.

The Miracle of Micro-Habits

The Buddha said, "Drop by drop, the water jug fills. Likewise, the wise one, gathering it little by little, fills themselves with good."[6] He didn't know it, but he was talking about what are now called micro-habits. A micro-habit is a small but meaningful step toward a big goal. Right now I'm employing micro-habits to help me learn Danish. Becoming fluent in that language is my big goal. My micro-habit—the drops I'm accumulating—is short sessions of just five or so minutes a day using a popular language-learning app. You might think that you wouldn't learn much in five minutes a day, but by the time I'd been practicing for about eighteen months I could often understand a fair bit of what the Danes I followed on social media were saying, and was able to decipher some of the headlines and summaries of news stories. After two years I was starting to join in with their conversations. So this is an example of a micro-habit—a small but meaningful step toward a larger goal. Drop by drop, my jar is filling.

Adopting micro-habits is a helpful strategy because one of our worst enemies when we're developing a new habit is naive optimism. Had I decided to learn Danish by studying for thirty minutes a day, I would have quickly given up. There are just too many days when I don't have that amount of time. Aiming for a lot of learning, I'd learn less. Aiming for a small amount of learning, I learn more.

In the meditation classes or sitting groups we attend, the sits are often twenty to forty minutes, or maybe even longer. When we try to establish a daily practice at home, we assume that's what we should do. And because we believe in willpower, we assume that if we *really* want to sit every day, it'll happen. But it's incredibly difficult to fit a new thirty- or forty-minute habit into an already full schedule. If you try, you're almost certainly setting yourself up for failure. *Merely wanting something to happen isn't enough. Setting a goal isn't enough.* Yes, you might manage to follow your lofty plans for a few days, but usually you'll find you can't sustain the effort. And then you'll feel bad and consider yourself a failure. And then you'll stop even trying, because you believe you don't have what it takes.

So I suggest the strategy of committing to meditate for just five minutes a day as a baseline for your practice. This is your micro-habit. These are your water drops. Five minutes of meditation a day is attainable; I think even the busiest of us can find five minutes each day for meditation. When you have the time and inclination you can of course meditate for longer, and maybe you'll do that most days. But it's almost inevitable that sometimes you're going to have a crazy schedule where five minutes is all you can manage, and you'll be glad you set the bar low. That day, you'll feel good about having succeeded at sticking to your commitment, while with a bigger aim you'd have failed and felt bad about it.

Now, some of you are going to say that a goal of five minutes a day is too little. That it's hardly worth it. That *real* meditation involves much longer sits. But remember that our goal is to establish a Rock-Solid Daily Meditation Habit. Five minutes a day gets your foot in the door; it allows you to have a daily practice. So we establish the daily habit first, *then* we're free to make the sits longer. In fact, I really hope you do end up meditating for thirty or forty minutes or more every single day—but if you want it to happen every day, start small and build up. If, after this exhortation, you're still skeptical about the wisdom of starting with five minutes of meditation a day, I have three words for you: *beware naive optimism*.

They say that the perfect is the enemy of the good. In my early days, long before I'd learned how to become a Rock-Solid Daily Meditator, I'd often not meditate at all if I couldn't sit for forty minutes. It would have been far better if I had settled for a shorter sit; if I'd said to myself, "I only have ten minutes to meditate, so I'll do ten minutes," rather than "I only have ten minutes to meditate, so I won't bother." Sitting for a shorter length of time would have kept the momentum of my practice going, and in the long run I'd have done far more meditation and felt much better about myself.

And I'm not alone with that. Countless people have fallen into the trap of this forty-minutes-or-nothing mindset, where spiritual perfectionism has prevented them from establishing a daily practice. Setting the bar low by committing to sit for at least five minutes a day is one of our most important strategies. Starting with a low bar gives you a feeling of success that you can build on. Starting with a high bar gives you a feeling of failure that stops you in your tracks.

This book is presented as a twenty-eight-day course, with one chapter for each day. Some days will introduce just one strategy, while some days will include several. The more strategies you have at your disposal, the more successful you're likely to be—so the further you get into the book, the more likely it is that you'll find yourself sitting daily. As you work your way through the book, you can intelligently adapt and fine-tune the strategies so that they fit your personal needs. Since accumulating a toolbox of strategies takes time, your meditation habit may not be rock solid from the very beginning. Early on you might miss a day now and then, but if that happens, don't lose heart. *Just keep on going.* Remember that this initial wobbliness is just part of the learning process. If you miss a day, just start sitting again as soon as possible. Reflect on what tripped you up and how you might do things differently next time. And above all, come back to the book and keep learning more strategies. Eventually you'll get to a tipping point where *you just don't miss days.*

By the time you get to Day 5 or 6 and have a decent number of strategies under your belt, I'm reasonably sure that most of you will already be more confident in your ability to do this. But it may take longer—maybe more than twenty-eight days. We're all different.

The Benefits of Daily Practice

There's no doubt that sitting daily improves the quality of your meditation practice. A couple of days off the cushion often leaves us with a backlog of emotional stuff to process. When you come back to your practice after a break you have to deal with this backlog, and your sits are distracted. If you continue sitting daily, however, then your practice settles down. Your mind becomes calmer. You're more at peace with yourself. And although your practice still has its ups and downs, as it always will, overall you'll feel that you're gathering momentum.

Meditating regularly also affects your experience in daily life. You know this. When you meditate, it makes you kinder and calmer. If you meditate consistently, you experience the benefits more consistently too. But there are other benefits as well. Charles Duhigg, a Pulitzer Prize–winning reporter who wrote a book called *The Power of Habit*, talks about the phenomenon of "keystone habits." These are good habits that help you to cultivate other good habits. The keystone is the highest stone in an arched bridge, and it holds all the other stones in place. No keystone, no bridge. With keystone habits in place, many other good habits can be supported. Meditation is a keystone habit. It supports the development of other good habits.

Every time I've run a Get Your Sit Together course, participants have reported that as they've learned to sit daily, they've developed other good habits as well. They start practicing a musical instrument they've neglected, or start running, or their houses become tidier. They are more attracted to healthy foods. This happens because one good habit—not just meditation, but regular, daily meditation—enables others to happen. Meditation tones down reactive emotions, making us less prone to the anxiety, depression, and anger that push us into making bad decisions. Meditation helps us be more focused and less distracted. It makes us more aware of what's truly important so that we can be more intentional in how we act in the world. It even promotes the growth of brain cells and improves your ability to think about complex things, making you smarter. All those things will help with any other good habit you may want to cultivate.

Perhaps the single most important benefit of establishing a regular daily practice, though, is confidence. Not being able to stick to our desire to meditate daily is undermining. But as the habit of meditating daily takes root, you start to feel a positive sense of accomplishment. You realize that you've overcome a pattern of resistance that's long defeated you. You feel more competent. You believe in yourself more and start to overcome self-doubts that have held you back in other areas of your life. Becoming a Rock-Solid Daily Meditator can be a profound turning point in our lives. It was for me, and I hope it will be for you too.

Two Ways to Use This Book

When I originally created the Get Your Sit Together program, it took the form of twenty-eight daily emails, each one of which contained a link to one or more guided meditations. There was also an online forum for discussion and support. The content of those emails, substantially rewritten, forms the basis of the twenty-eight chapters that await you. My first attempt to turn the program into a book consisted mainly of just those emails, with an added introduction and some supplementary material at the end. I wanted the book to be short and sweet, with brief chapters that you could read easily in a day. But that book, had it been published, would have been so slim that it would have vanished between the spines of the all the normal-sized books lining the shelves of your local bookshop. My publisher suggested expanding the book considerably. That was excellent advice, but it introduces the danger that if there's too much for you to read comfortably every day you might not be able to keep up. And then you might become demoralized and give up, which is the last thing I want.

This book is a support to help you meditate every day, and I don't want a lack of reading time to get in the way of your practice. So what I've done is to structure each chapter in six parts. If reading an entire chapter every day is too much, then don't read an entire chapter. Instead, you can focus each day on the material that's most central.

1. In each chapter there's a *Practice Reminder* section, which is just a few words reminding you of the importance of practicing meditation rather than merely reading about it. Reading about meditation can give us a virtuous feeling, even when we haven't actually done any practice. We want to avoid falling into that trap. If you find it helpful, listen to the guided meditations that you can find online here: https://wisdomexperience.org/sit-meditation-guides-from-bodhipaksa. Or just scan this QR code:

   These recordings can be a support for your practice.

2. Then there's a *Today* section. This offers a brief summary of what we're going to read on that day. So that's easy. If you don't have much time, just read these first two sections—Practice Reminder and Today—and *do your meditation practice*, with or without the support of the guided meditations.

3. Then there's the *Strategies* section, which offers suggestions to help you build the habit of meditating daily. These are the sections I recommend you make time to read if you can. I've kept them brief, so it should be easy enough to read one of these a day—but if that's not always possible, just do what you can. The main thing is to meditate.

4. Then there's a *Going Deeper* section, which explores the Buddhist teachings underpinning our practice. These are optional extras. If you don't have time to read them, then come back to them later. You might in effect end up reading the book twice—once for the stuff that gets you meditating daily, and a second time to add more depth to your understanding of what we're doing and why we're doing it.

5. There's a *Reflection* section, which encourages you to make the content of the Going Deeper section more experiential. The text is quite short, but journaling and reflecting can't always be hurried, so here again I suggest leaving this for days when you have plenty of time. Alternatively, you can come back to these exercises later.
6. Finally, each chapter ends with a *Last Words* section. This is usually just one or two sentences summarizing the Going Deeper section. If you don't have time to read the Going Deeper sections every day, at least you'll know what you're missing.

So, the two ways to read this book are to read it all in one go if you have the time, or to skip the Going Deeper bit and come back to it later if you don't.

One More Question (Actually It's Two)

Before we begin, I have an important question: *Is this a good time for you to start developing a daily meditation habit?* Sometimes it won't be. If you or your partner is giving birth tomorrow, for example, or if you have a huge project to do for work, or you're renovating your home, then this might not be a suitable time to get started. Sure, you will get to the point where you will keep practicing daily no matter what, but that's something we need to work toward. If it's not a good time, wait until life gets back to its usual levels of crazy, rather than off-the-charts crazy.

If nothing big is on the horizon, though, then perhaps this is as good a time as any to start becoming a Rock-Solid Daily Meditator. So I'll ask you another question: *Are you willing to commit to sit for five minutes every day?* Because that's the deal.

If the answer to both questions is yes, why not turn the page, and we'll get started.

DAY 1:

Track Your Practice

Practice Reminder

One of the problems people have in establishing a daily meditation practice is finding the time. Do you have five minutes right now? I assume you do, since you picked up this book with the intention to read it. Go sit! Practicing is *far* more important than reading about practicing. If you want, you can support your sit with one of the guided meditations available here: https://wisdomexperience.org/sit-meditation-guides-from-bodhipaksa. Or scan this QR code:

Today

Today we have something of a strategy dump, with several helpful things I encourage you to do: tapping into the power of celebration, recording your practice, changing your understanding of when a day begins and ends, and setting reminders.

Strategies

Celebrate

Assuming you just meditated, I'm going to ask you to do the following: Right now, say to yourself, out loud or in your head, "Yay, me!" Punch a fist in the air or raise both arms over your head, like a runner crossing the finish line. Celebration is important, because it creates pleasant feelings. Those feeling help you to feel good about practicing, making it more likely that you'll do it regularly. This is an important strategy that we'll explore further on Day 8, "Celebrate the Small Stuff."

Record Your Practice

Having a visual record of your practice is another powerful strategy for cultivating a Rock-Solid Daily Meditation Practice. Here's a link to a twenty-eight-day calendar that you can download and print out to track your progress: https://wisdomexperience.org/sit-meditation-guides-from-bodhipaksa. Or just scan this QR code:

If you already have a paper calendar (and if you've already meditated) you can put a big check mark on it for today. It helps if you have the calendar page in a place where you'll see it during the day.

Now you could in theory use a calendar on your computer or phone, but I do not recommend this. A phone calendar is not as immediately visible or accessible as a paper one that's taped to your refrigerator, and a more concrete reminder of your practice tends to be more effective. You have to remember to look at your phone's calendar before you can see it. If you forget, then it has failed as a reminder. Plus, phones themselves are a source of distraction.

What Is a "Day"?

We're aiming for a minimum of five minutes of meditation every day. I'd suggest that for the purpose of tracking your progress you define a day biologically, starting when you wake up and ending when you go back to sleep, rather than a calendar day, starting and ending at midnight.

The reason for defining days in this way is that some of us decide we're going to meditate before we go to sleep at night, but for whatever reason we stay up until after midnight. If it's 12:05 a.m. and you realize you haven't meditated since you got up, then from the point of view of the calendar, you've blown it. You missed a day. But from the point of view of human daily rhythms, it's still "today" and you can still meet your goal of meditating daily. Understanding a "day" in this way is an effective strategy.[7]

Set a Reminder

Allied with keeping a visual record of our meditation is the use of reminders. We like to think that we'll remember things, but our brains aren't very efficient, especially when they're juggling complex schedules. The human brain is essentially an electrochemical computer made of fat, protein, and water. It's a miracle that it can function at all, and it's not surprising that it is fallible. So set yourself some kind of reminder *right now*. It can be low-tech, like a sticky note by your bedside or on your bathroom mirror, or it can be more high-tech, like a repeating daily reminder on your phone. This is yet another strategy. Go do it. (Yes, I mean now.)

Assuming you've meditated today, your reminder should be to meditate for a minimum of five minutes tomorrow, preferably at a specified time. (We'll talk more about scheduling in tomorrow's chapter.)

We've already learned a lot of strategies, and it's only Day 1! There are a lot more of these tricks to come. That's all for now, except to say that if you haven't meditated yet today, make a detailed plan of when and where you're going to do it. Perhaps the time is now.

I recommend reading the following section only if you have the time. If not, skip it, move onto Day 2 tomorrow, and come back to read today's "Going Deeper" section at another time.

Going Deeper

The principle of conditionality, also known as dependent origination (*paṭiccasamuppāda* in Pali), is the essence of the Buddha's teaching, or Dharma. "Whoever sees conditionality sees the Dharma. Whoever sees the Dharma sees conditionality," he said.[8]

Conditionality means that things happen when—and only when—the conditions are right. To give an everyday example, a healthy plant arises in dependence upon water, as well as nutrients, air, appropriate temperatures, and so on. The healthy plant ceases to exist when any of those conditions is no longer present—as you've no doubt found if your ability to care for houseplants is anything like mine.

Conditionality means not just that things *only* happen when the conditions are right, but that they *will* happen when the conditions are right. Any given thing will inevitably come into being if the necessary supporting conditions are present. With the appropriate conditions, a seed *will* develop into a healthy plant. If it doesn't, then some condition was missing.

Now, if we want to create a regular daily meditation practice, we often assume that the most important supportive condition is willpower, because that's what we've been told all our lives. But willpower—forcing yourself to do something you're resistant to—is not the answer. The importance of willpower is something that the Buddha seems to have had fun debunking. One time he conjured up a scenario that I imagine gave his monks a good chuckle:

> *Suppose a man were to throw a large boulder into a deep lake of water, and a great crowd of people, gathering and congregating, would pray, praise, and circumambulate with their hands palm-to-palm over the heart [saying], "Rise up, O boulder! Come floating up, O boulder! Come float to the shore, O boulder!" What do you think: would that boulder—because of the prayers, praise, and circumambulation of that great crowd of people—rise up, come floating up, or come float to the shore?*[9]

The monks reportedly said "No, Lord." (Although some of them might have been thinking, "Is this a trick question?")

The Buddha repeatedly pointed out that wishing for something to happen is a fruitless exercise unless we take the appropriate practical steps to produce the desired outcome. He emphasized that spiritual practice will be successful even when we don't have an overt wish for success, as long as we're doing the right things. "If they follow the holy life even when having made no wish, they are capable of obtaining results ... Why is that? Because it is an appropriate way of obtaining results."[10]

This book is based on the principle of conditionality. To become Rock-Solid Daily Meditators we need to adopt strategies that help create and sustain a daily meditation practice. These are habits that bring your practice to mind, make you keen to practice, and make it easier to meditate than not to meditate. Of course we need to *want* to meditate daily. The desire to meditate daily is a necessary condition for success. But that desire is not sufficient in itself. The idea behind willpower is that all you need is the desire, and that success comes from making the desire stronger. (Honestly, it's exhausting just writing about it!) So, having the desire is a necessary starting point, but no amount of desire is going to bring about significant change in the absence of strategic action.

So, in this twenty-eight-day program, we're engaged in a practical exploration of conditionality. What conditions—actions or outlooks—support the arising of a Rock-Solid Daily Meditation Practice? What conditions hinder us, and how can we learn to avoid them? Exploring these topics, and putting the lessons we learn into practice, is the purpose of this book.

Today we've learned the importance of several of those conditions: prioritizing practice over reading about practice, keeping a visual reminder of our progress, creating reminders, and thinking of days as being organic rather than dictated by the calendar. That's already a lot, and we'll learn many more supportive conditions over the rest of this twenty-eight-day program.

Conditionality, as well as being the general principle that things exist only if we create the appropriate conditions, is often formulated in the early Buddhist teachings as lists of experiences leading from suffering to enlightenment. Meditation and the states arising from it are frequently a part of these formulas. Without going into too much detail, a common pattern in these spiritual flow charts is that living ethically (that is, with kindness and mindfulness) leads to freedom from remorse, making it easier for us to meditate. Meditation in turn leads to joy, ease, and calm, bringing about a deep stillness that makes it easier for us to observe our experience closely. And this close observation of our experience—especially its impermanent and insubstantial nature—leads to awakening, or enlightenment, which is freedom from suffering.[11]

It's good to remember, then, that in creating the habit of daily meditation, we are also creating a life that's more joyful and satisfying, and that leads toward enlightenment. Right now, right here, you're on a path that leads to Buddhahood. And you're not alone. We'll be together every step of the way.

Reflection

Spend some time thinking about a good habit that you already do regularly. It might be something like going to the gym or learning a language on an app. Write down all the conditions you can think of that support that practice. If I were to write about brushing my teeth, I might list things like "It's part of my morning bathroom routine. The toothbrush and toothpaste are right there in front of me. I enjoy running my tongue over my smooth, clean teeth." And so on. Write down *everything*, no matter how trivial it may seem. If you do something regularly, there are probably lots of supportive conditions.

Last Words

One by one we put into place the conditions that support the creation of a Rock-Solid Daily Meditation Practice. We need to want to establish that habit, but wanting is not enough. What's important is that we intelligently work to make sure that every internal and external factor we can work with is designed to support rather than hinder our desire to meditate daily.

See you tomorrow!

DAY 2

Have a Plan B

Practice Reminder

Remember to sit for at least five minutes. If you want, use one of the guided meditations that you can sign up to receive at this link: https://wisdomexperience.org/sit-meditation-guides-from-bodhipaksa. Or just scan this QR code:

Remember to celebrate afterward, and to record your progress on your calendar. These are all supportive conditions for establishing a Rock-Solid Daily Meditation Practice.

Today

Now, we'll be looking at another powerful supporting condition, which is for you to plan your practice and—crucially—to plan what you'll do if your original plan goes sideways.

Strategies

Let's see what we can learn from a scientific study about encouraging good habits. The study was about how medical professionals can encourage people recovering from heart attacks to do more exercise.

Getting yourself to exercise is hard. You'd think that a brush with death would be motivation enough, but habits are hard to change. To find out what worked best, the researchers divided their cardiac patients into three groups:

1. A *control group*, who were simply recommended to exercise.
2. An *action planning group*, who were asked to plan specifically when, where, and how they intended to exercise.
3. A *combined planning group*, who received the same instructions as the action planning group, but who were also asked to anticipate possible obstacles to exercising and how they would overcome them.

In other words, the first group had no plan. The second group had a plan A. And the third group had a plan A and also a plan B to fall back on.

The control group averaged 95 minutes of exercise each week. The action planning group did much better, averaging 113 minutes. Planning is helpful!

But the combined planning group—the ones who had both a plan A and a plan B—did an average of 179 minutes of exercise each week.[12] That's almost double the exercise done by the control group and almost 60 percent more than the action planning group. Planning is good, but planning for the failure of your plan is even better!

Here's how we can use this insight in building a daily meditation habit.

1. Plan Your Practice

First, take a few minutes right now to think about these questions: When are you planning to meditate next? Where do you plan to do it? Will it be guided or unguided? If guided, what meditation are you using? For how long will you sit? And (if applicable) with whom do you plan to meditate?

The more precise your plans, the more helpful they will be. Writing them down will help you to remember them.

2. Then Plan It Again

Now, create a plan B that covers what you'll do if something interferes with your meditation plans. You don't have to anticipate every potential problem. You just need to plan what your fallback position is if your first plan doesn't work out for whatever reason. This plan should cover the same things as before: when, where, how, for how long, and with whom you plan to meditate.

If plan A—which might have been to meditate at 8:30 a.m. in your bedroom, for ten minutes, without guidance—doesn't work out, maybe your plan B is that you sneak off to a conference room at work at 1:00 p.m. and meditate for five minutes using a guided meditation from an app. Or maybe you'll decide that you'll meditate in the train on the way home, wearing headphones. Or that you'll meditate sitting upright in bed just before you go to sleep. We've already seen that reminders are useful, so whatever the details of your plan B are, you might want to put them in your planner.

Besides the fact that having a plan B is helpful, there's another important lesson in this: if your plan A is to meditate last thing at night before bed, then you don't have a plan B. If you forget to sit, there won't be a second chance, because it'll be the morning by the time you realize you've forgotten, and by then it's too late; you've already missed a day. (Sorry, there's only so far we can stretch the big ball of wibbly-wobbly, timey-wimey stuff that we call "a day.") So, planning to meditate earlier in the day is better, purely from a practical standpoint.

Related to this, if you meditate in bed (as plan B) before you go to sleep, do it sitting upright. If you meditate lying on your back, you will probably fall asleep, which is a time-honored way of failing to meditate daily. Falling asleep is far less likely if you sit upright for your "beditations." (Please don't blame me. I didn't invent this term!)

So, you have learned four more strategies: planning your meditations, planning a fallback position in case something goes wrong, not having your plan A be just before bed (although that's acceptable for a plan B), and not meditating lying down in bed, unless it doesn't matter that you fall asleep.

Going Deeper

My first girlfriend at college told me that when she went out on the town, she preferred to take a less attractive friend with her, because strangers would pay more attention to her than to her friend. That sounded like an excellent strategy! It turns out that mindfulness (*sati*) has a less attractive friend, called *sampajañña*. Almost daily there are newspaper and magazine articles touting the benefits of mindfulness. There are thousands of science papers written about it every year. You can even buy mindfulness coloring books. All eyes are on mindfulness—which is a shame, because *sampajañña* has a *great* personality.

Perhaps one of the reasons *sampajañña* is not so well known is that you can read six different translations of the Buddhist texts, and it's rendered differently each time. It's been translated as "awareness," "introspection," "clear comprehension," "full awareness," "alertness," "clear knowledge," and "situational awareness," to name but a few variants. You could read all these different terms and not realize that they point back to the same original word. I apologize for adding yet another translation, but I'm going to refer to *sampajañña* as "intentionality," for reasons I'll explain shortly.

Mindfulness is about observing what's going on in the present moment. It involves being aware of what we're sensing, feeling, thinking, and doing. *Sampajañña* takes a wider view and sees how what's going on in the present moment relates to the past and future. You can think of *sati* as being about observing and *sampajañña* as being about monitoring, with the connotation of comparing a current state to a state that's desired. I'll offer an anecdote to explain this. It's a story I heard a long time ago, from an Insight Meditation teacher I'll call Susan, which may actually have been her real name.

Susan was on retreat, and she was practicing walking meditation outside of the retreat building. This is the kind of walking meditation that is very slow: lifting one foot and moving it forward in preparation for moving the next foot might take a minute or two. She was deeply into her senses, completely focused in the moment. She observed many sensations from the body, from the pressure of her feet on the gravel of the driveway, to the slow movements of muscles shifting, to the breath flowing in and out. Birds sang. The gravel crunched slowly. And then, gently at first, a deep vibration began to arise. Growing, it became an intense, resonant thrum. Slow pace after slow pace it became stronger, until the air, the earth itself, and even her body trembled, reverberated, and pulsated. This new and fascinating sensation was both in the world and in her body—an all-encompassing phenomenon. The whole cosmos was vibrating. Was this some kind of awakening experience? A realization of the vibrational nature of reality? No, she realized, as insight dawned: It was the engine of a delivery truck in the driveway, which she'd been walking toward as it arrived, and whose radiator grill was now mere inches in front of her.

This lovely story, which Susan so generously told in a wonderfully self-deprecating manner, was an excellent example of how you can be so mindful that you're, in a way, unmindful. According to Bhikkhu Anālayo, the "cooperation of mindfulness with clear knowledge [*sampajañña*] . . . points to the need to combine mindful observation of phenomena with an intelligent processing of the observed data."[13] Mindfulness is being present with what's arising. It involves observing—for example, noticing all the sensations that arise as you walk. *Sampajañña* is knowing what all that's *about*. How, for example, does what's going on right now relate to your goals? You might know what you're thinking—that's mindfulness—but is that the best thing to be thinking about right now? You might know how you're feeling, but is the way you're feeling helpful or unhelpful? You're aware of thrumming sounds, but do you recognize that they are coming from a truck, and is walking into it what you want to be doing?

Intentionality, or *sampajañña*, involves setting intentions—such as the intention to meditate daily—and remaining aware of and true to them. Today's suggestion is to employ intentionality strategically, so that we don't just plan our meditation, but we also plan what we'll do if our plans fall through. This helps us to stick with our intention.

Incidentally, one of the great advantages of meditating in the morning is that having fulfilled your intention, you can simply let go of it. If I plan to meditate later in the day, I'm often visited by a nagging voice saying, "Have you meditated yet? No, you haven't! Don't forget to meditate!" Once you've done your daily practice, you're less likely to be troubled by that voice. And if it does pipe up, it's great to be able to tell it that you have that covered. It's a real relief just to get your practice out of the way.

Sampajañña is involved at all levels of spiritual practice. Ethics, for example, involves comparing how we're behaving with how we would ideally behave. For example, we might find that we're getting irritated with someone, realize how unhelpful that is, and muster our reserves of patience and kindness, because that's how we'd rather live. Monitoring—making a comparison between where you're at and where you want to be—brings about a course correction. In meditation, intentionality keeps an eye on whether the mind is straying from the purpose of the practice. (When we're distracted a lot of the time in our sits, we might think it's mindfulness that we need to develop, but more often it's *sampajañña* that's lacking.)

Sampajañña is also involved in cultivating insight. As Bhikkhu Anālayo puts it, "'to clearly know' can be taken to represent the 'illuminating' or 'awakening' aspect of contemplation."[14] The Buddha described the practice of *sampajañña* as follows: "It's when a mendicant knows feelings . . . thoughts . . . and perceptions as they arise, as they remain, and as they vanish."[15] Here the word *intentionality* means "maintaining the intention to see things as they really are." This is an intention we can develop alongside the intention to meditate daily. Enlightenment is, after all, the ultimate aim of all practice.

Reflection

In your next meditation, see if you can not only observe the breathing (or whatever you're paying attention to) but also be aware of your intention to do so. This creates a more complex experience: You're aware of your experience and you're also aware that it's your intention to be aware of your experience. You can be aware whether that intention is present or has gone missing. Afterward, write a few notes about how this added complexity changes your practice.

Last Words

To sustain a daily meditation practice, we need to exert intentionality. Once again, this isn't merely a matter of willpower. Rather, we formulate a plan, and support ourselves in turning that plan into reality by using reminders. We find that planning—and acting on our plans—helps to strengthen our power of intentionality, so that it becomes a recurring check: *Have I meditated yet today?*

DAY 3

Master the Hindrance in Your Pocket

Practice Reminder

Plan when you're going to sit. Maybe that could be now? If you haven't meditated yet, make a plan B, just in case. Keep up the habit of sitting for at least five minutes, celebrate ("Yay, me!"), and then make a visual record of your practice. You can use a guided meditation to support you, if you find that helpful.

Today

Now we'll discuss one of the main modern-day hindrances to meditation—your smartphone—and strategies to stop it getting in the way of your daily practice.

Strategies

Today I want to discuss one particularly pernicious hindrance to practice: your smartphone. Modern phones are small rectangles made of glass, metal, silicon—and craving.

Because our phones are now our alarm clocks, the first physical object we touch in the morning is often a glowing screen bombarding us with information about the various emails, text messages, social media activity, and app notifications that have piled up overnight. It's easy to get sucked into all that and to find that your meditation time has evaporated into a cloud of pixels. Now, you could try to treat this as a "willpower" problem and fight your urges, but we all know how well that works. So instead, let's look at how you can be strategic.

What if you were to use an inexpensive alarm clock instead of your phone to wake yourself up? That way you can turn your phone off overnight, and not be bombarded with distractions first thing. The fact that checking your notifications in the morning requires turning your phone on and then waiting while the device reboots then works to your advantage. You've introduced friction into the system. Friction in this sense means making it a little harder to get distracted, which makes it a little easier for you to recall and follow through on your intention to sit. You can meditate before turning your phone on, but if you do turn your phone on before meditation, the fact that you did so as a conscious act makes it more likely that you'll go straight to a meditation app. Establishing a moment of mindfulness and intentionality first thing in the morning, rather than diving into mindless scrolling, is a powerful thing.

If you're nervous about turning your phone off overnight just in case there's some kind of emergency, you can keep it on but charge it on the other side of the room. Again, this introduces some friction, because you have time to summon your reserves of mindfulness and intentionality before you touch your phone.

I found these principles helpful when I wanted to break my addiction to social media. Realizing that Facebook, Twitter, and so on were consuming a huge amount of my time, I used strategies like these to make those apps harder to access. I used other strategies, too, such as removing the apps from my phone. Eventually I got to the point where I realized that I was happier not using those services, and so I deleted my accounts. Having broken those addictions, I find it much easier to get onto the cushion. That's not the result of willpower; it's because I've developed strategies that make it easier to meditate than not to meditate.

Going Deeper

"All of man's misfortune comes from one thing, which is not knowing how to sit quietly in a room," observed Blaise Pascal. Writing as he did some 350 years before the invention of the smartphone, I think it's safe to say that he did not know the half of it.

We're so addicted to stimulation that in one study run by the University of Virginia, 67 percent of men and 25 percent of women who had been deprived of their phones chose to give themselves painful electric shocks rather than sit quietly in a room with only their own thoughts for company.[16] Incredible, isn't it? This is the result of the companies that design apps—especially social media apps—having put an enormous amount of research into how to make their services as addictive as possible. They know all about craving and how to stimulate it.

With our intentionality hijacked by social media apps, we're depriving ourselves of sleep, making ourselves depressed by comparing ourselves to the carefully curated, "perfect" lives that others share online, and are seemingly unable to have an idle moment without picking up our devices and checking our notifications. We find ourselves getting drawn into heated arguments. We get anxious at the mere thought of being offline. Sometimes our minds become so restless that we lose the ability to stay focused on the simple task of reading a book. (That last one was the deal-breaker for me. It's made me realize I had to curb my social media use.)

The Buddha also studied craving, but for a different reason: He wanted to help us become free from the suffering it causes. The Pali for craving is *taṇhā*, which literally means "thirst." If you recall the experience of restlessly picking up your phone, it does rather resemble the behavioral tic of restlessly sipping a drink. But while drinking water will slake our physical thirst, picking up our phones and browsing social media does nothing to slake our psychological thirst. It's like sipping salt water. Usually we only stop when we become bored, or tired, or disgusted. Or maybe we only stop because our schedule demands that we go do something else.

What is this psychological thirst that we so often experience? Why does it cause us to reach for our phones? And why do our phones do such a poor job of satisfying it? The Buddha pointed out that beneath our desires—like the urge to browse social media—are *feelings*. Usually the feelings that provoke social media use are unpleasant. The next time you feel the compelling urge to pick up your phone, pause and notice what you're experiencing in your body. Pay particular attention to the areas around the heart, the diaphragm, and the belly. Those are where our most important feelings tend to manifest. You might sense a hollowness, or a tight knot of tension, or a buzzing, tingling feeling. Or it may be something else. The key thing, though, is that the feeling has an unpleasant quality to it. Because it's unpleasant, we want to get rid of it or escape from it. And that's why we're motivated to pick up our phones. We're trying to numb or outrun our own unpleasant feelings.

When he taught the principle of conditionality we discussed on Day 1, the Buddha said, "In dependence upon feeling arises craving." Now the Buddha was remarkably single-minded in his teaching. Everything he said comes back to suffering, and how to escape suffering. How does knowing that craving arises from feeling help us? Well, if you do that experiment of catching yourself in the act of picking up your phone, notice what you're experiencing in the body, and choose to remain mindful of those feelings, then you'll notice that your craving begins to weaken. It might even die away altogether.

If you simply continue to be mindful of the unpleasant feeling for as long as it lasts, you will begin to realize that you can be content with that experience. Your body and mind can contain the unpleasant sensation, and around it you can experience contentment, happiness, and peace. You start to understand that you don't need your phone to help you escape unpleasant feelings. You understand that your phone can't really help you escape discomfort; at best it can help you to push it out of awareness for a little while. You understand that you don't need to escape unpleasant feelings at all. You can just experience them until they pass.

Your craving—your thirst to escape unpleasant feelings—is not very effective as a strategy, and is in fact even counterproductive. You can observe this in your own experience. How do you feel after a long session of scrolling through social media? You probably don't feel satisfied or at peace. In fact, you're probably at least as dissatisfied and restless as you were before, but maybe with some disgust added in. The things we expose ourselves to on social media—from the comparisons with other people's apparently perfect lives, to the bad news and squabbles we're bombarded with—not only don't relieve us of the unpleasant feelings we started with, but they add to them. Social media is a "solution" to suffering that causes yet more suffering.

The Buddha pointed out that conditionality can be cyclical. We start off suffering, in the sense that we have uncomfortable feelings, and we respond with "thirsty" actions that lead to further suffering. To suffer less, we need to break that cycle. We need to take things in a different direction. We need to train ourselves to respond to unpleasant feelings with mindfulness and intentionality, *sati* and *sampajañña*. And as we do so, we start to free ourselves from the compulsive, mindless behaviors that make us suffer.

This too is conditionality. It's a form of conditionality that, rather than causing suffering, frees us from it. It does, as Pascal says, allow us to "sit quietly in a room" (without needing to give ourselves electric shocks), but it goes much further than that. The Buddha described liberative conditionality as ultimately leading us to spiritual awakening. In the meantime, though, it can be a tool to free us from the compulsion to browse our phones so much that we have no time left to meditate.

Reflection

For perhaps just one morning, afternoon, or evening, let the act of picking up and putting down your phone be a mindfulness prompt. Note how you were feeling just before you picked up your device. Were you bored? Restless? Anxious? Overwhelmed? Excited? At ease? Note how you feel each time you put your phone down again. Is it easy to disengage from your phone? Is it hard? How do you feel afterward? Are you fulfilled? Do you feel a yearning to stay online, or is there a sense of relief in extracting yourself from the digital world? Write down the details of each encounter.

Last Words

Bear in mind that no matter how powerful your cravings are, you always have some degree of choice about how to act. There is always at least a little wiggle room in your life to help you escape craving and the suffering it leads to. It takes time and practice, but the more you exercise mindfulness and intentionality, the easier it becomes.

DAY 4

Tap Into the Power of Rewards

Practice Reminder

Remember to sit for at least five minutes, to celebrate afterward, and to record your progress on your calendar. The act of celebrating is important because it helps you feel good about your practice, and this is helpful if you feel bad about repeatedly failing to create consistency.

Today

Let's talk about rewards, how to create them, and why they're helpful.

Strategies

Every habit has three parts: a cue, an action, and a reward. Maybe the cue is that you're feeling bored; the action is that you make and eat popcorn; and the reward is the ritual of munching on a tasty, crunchy snack. Or maybe the cue is when you start to feel tired while working; the action is that you check Facebook; the reward is seeing that people have taken an interest in your posts. Do these things once, and it's just something you've done. Repeat those three steps over and over, and they become automatic. You no longer think about what you're doing, and it may even be hard to stop yourself. That's a habit.

Today, let's focus on the rewards. Popcorn is rewarding because it tastes nice. Facebook is rewarding (sometimes) because it reminds us that other people are interested in us, or because we see cute videos of cats, or because it gives us a break from a boring task. What's the reward with meditation? Now, meditation *can* be intrinsically rewarding—that is, the act of meditating itself can sometimes make you feel good. But often meditation is difficult, and so it's not *reliably* rewarding. And even when your meditation is enjoyable, that may not be enough to motivate you to do it. There are, after all, lots of competing habits that can more readily give you rewards—watching TV or surfing the internet, for example. So we need to consciously reward ourselves for meditating.

But how do we reward ourselves? Take ourselves out for a nice meal? Buy a new pair of shoes? Crack open a bottle of champagne? Obviously, those things wouldn't be practical to do every day. What I suggest is simply that you *celebrate*. We feel good when we congratulate ourselves. If we say, "Yay me!" or "Good job for meditating! That was an excellent thing to do! Keep it up!" this makes us feel good. It's the pleasure that results from congratulation that becomes our reward. And we need that reward so we can make meditation into a daily habit.

Making physical gestures is a powerful way of heightening the pleasure of celebration. We can punch the air or raise our arms over our heads in victory. Those gestures naturally trigger reward chemicals in the brain, making us feel good. So we meditate, celebrate, and feel good. The pleasant feelings we evoke make it more likely we'll return to the cushion.

Even just anticipating rewards brings rewards. It makes us feel happy right now. Imagine the difference between thinking, "I haven't meditated yet. Ugh!" and "I haven't meditated yet. Think how good I'm going to feel after I put that big check mark in my calendar!" The first makes it more likely we won't meditate at all. The second doubles our reward: We feel good now and we'll feel good later. And whether we make ourselves feel good through pleasant anticipation or bad through self-criticism is up to us. It's a choice.

Now, some of you will have been brought up to be bashful about celebrating yourselves. Maybe you were raised to think it's boastful to celebrate achievements. But celebrating the fact that you've meditated isn't going to inflate your ego. It's just going to help you meditate, which will in turn make you a less self-centered person. Now it may take a while for you to overcome your natural reluctance to celebrate. But keep going "Yay, me!" and it'll happen.

Going Deeper

When the Buddha said, "What a practitioner dwells upon becomes the inclination of their mind,"[17] he was talking about developing habits. In the languages he spoke there was a word that means something very similar to our word "habit." In Pali it's *saṅkhāra*, which means, in a psychological context, both "a behavior built up through repetition" and also "building a tendency to behave in a certain way through repetition." He was very familiar with the concept that habits are built up through repeated action.

The Buddha, however, certainly didn't have a word for *neuron*, and without a great deal of explanation wouldn't have understood what neuroscientists mean when they say, "Neurons that fire together, wire together," which is just a different way of talking about habits. Patterns of activity in the brain become more and more entrenched when those patterns are repeatedly triggered. Repetition is what builds habits.

Now, when we're working on building a daily meditation habit, we're not just creating a new habit; we're also having to unlearn old ones. We're undoing old *saṅkhāras*. We have existing habits that interfere with developing new ones. These include habitual feelings of disappointment that might have become associated with our meditation practice. When we've struggled and failed to build up a daily meditation habit, we start to feel bad about ourselves as meditators. We come to think of meditation as an area of life where we keep failing, and this triggers shame and disappointment.

We need to do something about the tendency to have those feelings if we want to build a Rock-Solid Daily Meditation Habit. And to change the emotional tone connected with our meditation practice we can celebrate the very fact of sitting, as I've described above. Celebrating that we've meditated creates pleasant feelings. Celebrating over and over creates habitual associations, so that you start to feel good about meditating. Because neurons that fire together wire together, those pleasant feelings become deeply connected with our practice. We start to feel good about daily practice. And as we eradicate the old, unhelpful associations that we'd previously built up, we start to feel good about ourselves as practitioners.

I've mentioned that celebration can be physical as well as verbal. When you feel good, you naturally make celebratory gestures. We all know that runners raise their arms over their heads in a gesture of victory when they cross the finishing line. What's particularly fascinating is that even runners who have been blind from birth will do this, despite never having seen anyone else do it. This just goes to show how instinctual and deeply rooted such gestures are in our evolutionary history.

The connection works the other way around as well. When you make celebratory gestures, you naturally feel good. This is because the "feeling good" neurons and the "making expansive gestures" neurons, being wired together, fire together. This is why I recommend that you not just celebrate verbally by saying things like "Yay, me!" but also raise your arms over your head in a gesture of victory. This action automatically triggers the release of hormones such as testosterone, which make you feel confident, and it decreases the production of stress hormones such as cortisol, which make you feel bad.[18]

On a related note, it's important that we pay close attention to the way we sit in meditation, because of the principle that how we hold our bodies affects how we feel, and even how the mind functions. Studies show that when we slump, we feel less alert. It also becomes harder for us to recall pleasant and comforting memories, and easier to dredge up memories that make us feel unhappy. Slumping makes us sleepy and depressed. When we slump during meditation, even in relatively subtle ways, we create the conditions for unpleasant experiences to arise. In contrast, when we adopt a posture that's upright and open, the mind becomes clearer and more alert, and it becomes easier for us to access more pleasant memories. In meditation, this helps us to have more confidence, and calmer, more enjoyable sits.

These effects are by no means insignificant. I remember meditating one night before a crucial presidential election. I was feeling anxious, and I made a particular point of sitting in an open and upright way. I realized for the first time that while meditating I tended to let my elbows rest against my sides, and I remembered that on Buddha statues you can often see a triangle of daylight between the arms and the side of the body. So I put just a little more energy into my arms, so that the elbows moved way from my sides and I took up a little bit more space. To an external observer, the difference would have been barely noticeable, but from the inside, the change in my experience was profound. My anxiety quickly settled, and a powerful sense of confidence arose. As I turned my mind back to the matter of the election, I realized that a stable state of equanimity had arisen, to the point that however the election turned out, my sense of well-being would not be affected.

So I suggest you play with these things and observe the ways in which your posture and sense of well-being are connected. This will help you to develop strong feelings of confidence, contentment, and joy, and to associate these qualities with your meditation practice, so that you feel drawn to your sitting practice rather than to avoiding it.

Reflection

One way to bring more joy into life is to consciously express gratitude. Take some time to think about five things you're grateful for, and write them down. If you have trouble thinking of anything, then simply look around you and notice things that you would miss if they weren't in your life. Don't list things mechanically; hold each of the things you're grateful for in your heart until you feel at least the glimmerings of joy and appreciation. This is something I do every morning. You might want to consider adopting this practice as well.

Last Words

To evoke pleasant feelings, celebrate, both verbally and physically, at the end of every period of practice. Don't save celebrations for "good sits," whatever that might mean. Instead, *celebrate the very fact that you sat*. Also, try sitting just a little more upright and with a little more expansiveness. When your mind associates your practice with pleasure, it will be automatically drawn to sitting.

DAY 5

Change Your Self-View

Practice Reminder

Remember to sit for at least five minutes, to celebrate afterward, and to record your progress on your calendar.

Today

We all carry around a self-view, which is a picture we've built up that tells the story of who we are, what we're good at and bad at, whether we are worthy, and so on. Those self-views can become traps that limit us, but it's within our power to create more liberating and empowering stories about ourselves.

Strategies

Back when I struggled to keep my practice regular, I knew that my life was much better when I meditated regularly: I was a calmer, happier, less anxious, friendlier person. And yet knowing that didn't help much in getting me on the cushion every day. I had even learned lots about the benefits of meditation by reading scientific studies. I learned, for example, that meditating keeps you healthier, reduces stress, promotes happiness, slows the aging in your brain, and reduces pain. I assumed that knowing all this would help motivate me to sit daily. But it didn't.

Repeatedly failing to establish a daily meditation practice affects how you see yourself. You start to assume there's something wrong with you. You think you lack commitment, discipline, willpower, or faith in your practice. Those self-views become firmly established, so that you come to believe that you are just *not the kind of person who can meditate daily*. And this becomes a self-fulfilling prophecy; if you believe you're incapable of meditating daily, you almost certainly won't be able to.

Let's do something about that.

I'm going to share the tool that, more than any other, has helped me and many other people to establish a Rock-Solid Daily Meditation Habit. It's surprisingly simple: just keep repeating to yourself the words "I meditate every day. It's just what I do. It's part of who I am." Repeating this mantra reprograms your sense of who you are. You start to see yourself as someone who meditates daily without fail. One of my meditation students, Andrea, said something many other people have said: "I was so tempted to skip today, but I remembered that *I meditate every day*." After just three weeks of repeating this mantra, she had internalized the message to the point where it had changed how she saw herself—and her commitment to her practice. For Andrea, skipping meditation was no longer an option. That was no longer the kind of person she was. Here too, the phrase becomes a self-fulfilling prophecy, but this time in a positive sense. The mantra motivates you to sit. This is what I consider to be the most important of all the tools that I am sharing with you in this book. It gets right to the heart of our problem in establishing a daily practice: our belief that we can't.

Now, there are a few things you need to bear in mind about using this mantra. To encourage these phrases to sink in it's helpful to repeat them *a lot*. Say them to yourself when you first wake up in the morning. Say them in the shower. Say them while you're driving or sitting on public transport. Say them while you're washing the dishes; in the gym; while walking; while you're lying in bed waiting to fall asleep. Say them at the start and end and even in the middle of your meditation practice. Bombard your mind with this message. Drum it in.

You might be thinking, "But that's not true. I don't meditate every day." Now, not wanting to repeat an untrue statement is a valid ethical concern, so if this is a problem for you then maybe it's best to wait until you've meditated for several consecutive days before adopting this mantra. *Then* it'll be true. Or think about it as an intention for the present and the future.

Don't assume that the mantra is somehow going to do all the work for you. You still need to commit to sit, and to intelligently use whatever strategies you need so you can follow through on that commitment. Do whatever it takes. But if you keep repeating the mantra, you'll find that it supports and amplifies your intention.

The mantra becomes a self-fulfilling prophecy. You meditate every day because you're a person who meditates every day. It's just what you want to do. Meditating daily is part of who you are. You don't even think about it. You don't need willpower to sit every day any more than you need willpower to brush your teeth every day. You just do it.

Your self-view has changed, and so have you. Just remember: "I meditate every day. It's just what I do. It's part of who I am."

Going Deeper

We all pick up self-limiting views about ourselves as we grow up. These views can either narrow or widen what we believe we're capable of. We jump from "this doesn't come easily to me" or "this might be difficult" to "I can't do this, and I'm not even going to try."

A self-limiting view I often hear is "I could never meditate. My mind's too busy." As a meditation teacher I know that meditation is not about settling into some blissful state of calm, but instead about sitting with your experience, whatever that may be. So what if your mind is busy? That's why we sit! Since you're reading this book you probably don't have the "I can't meditate" view, but you probably have the "I can't meditate every day" view. And the "I lack the willpower" view. And the "Other people can do it, but I can't" view. These stories we tell ourselves seem utterly convincing, but in fact they're just stories. They're not reality—because we haven't yet discovered what we're capable of.

Self-limiting stories can be a way of avoiding the frustration that often accompanies learning new skills. We might fancy that if we take piano lessons we'll soon be surprising and delighting people at parties as we slide behind the keyboard and produce rippling melodies, only to have our illusions shattered as we struggle to clunk our way around basic scales. The fact that the reality of learning is so different from our fantasy is disappointing. And sometimes others will ridicule our efforts, which makes an already challenging situation into a humiliating ordeal. To spare ourselves this unpleasantness it's easier if we simply tell ourselves, "I can't do this. I've tried, and I just don't have the skill. It's just not me." So we stop.

Or we're told at our first meditation class, after being guided through a couple of twenty- or thirty-minute sits, "Remember to set aside time to meditate every day." So we try to find twenty or thirty minutes in our already packed schedule and find that there is no free time just sitting there waiting to be claimed, or that other things like TV or social media demand our attention more strongly than our practice does. Or maybe by force of will we cram in a long sit for a couple of days, but find that carving out the time to meditate causes more stress than the meditation relieves us of. Or we just forget. Over years of faltering attempts, this mythical *remembering to set aside time to meditate every day* never quite happens. And we develop a view that it doesn't happen because we can't do it.

Fortunately, it's possible for us to change our self-views. If we recognize that our limiting views are just stories, then we can see that we don't have to believe them. We can change them, or practice adopting other, more empowering stories. And this is exactly what we're doing when we start saying to ourselves "I meditate every day. It's just what I do. It's part of who I am."

This too becomes a self-view, but in an enabling, empowering way. It's a helpful view that allows us to transcend the limits we've imposed upon ourselves. We contemplate skipping meditation, but remember "I meditate every day." And so we do sit. We just want to. It's just what we do. We give ourselves permission to grow. Prediction becomes reality. Using the power of a consciously chosen self-view, we become and remain a Rock-Solid Daily Meditator.

Reflection

Make some notes on the views you hold about yourself as a meditator. You can include the good ("I bring creativity into my practice") and the not-so-good ("I forget to practice when I'm busy"). Try to drill down to the core views that get in the way of you meditating every day without fail. Take those beliefs and reflect on how they might function as self-fulfilling prophecies that stop you meditating regularly. If you recognize that these views no longer serve you, then write down new, more empowering beliefs that support your goals. "I meditate every day. It's just what I do. It's part of who I am" might be enough, but perhaps you can find other ways to say this that resonate more strongly with you.

Last Words

You've developed views about who you are and what you're capable of. Some of those views may be helpful, but some may be very unhelpful indeed. Fortunately, you've also inherited the ability to change how you see yourself. You developed those unhelpful views, and you can lose them too. You can choose to embrace healthier, more realistic views about yourself that enable you to grow and flourish.

DAY 6

Keep Yourself Accountable

Practice Reminder

Remember to sit, to congratulate yourself, and to record your practice. Don't break the chain!

Today

Today, let's look at how we can get motivation from sharing our progress with apps, friends, or a community—and even through self-blackmail.

Strategies

You can support your desire to sit daily with the help of planning, visual tracking, celebrating, and repeating phrases that reprogram your sense of self. But social motivational factors are helpful too. We behave more honestly if we perceive we're being observed. For example, in churches where congregants and visitors pay for votive candles on an honor system, putting a poster with someone's face on it beside the donation box reduces the number of people who take candles without paying.

Exposing our practice to the gaze of other people can help motivate us to show up. The "other" can even be something like an app. I've mentioned that I'm spending time every day learning Danish. The app I use sends me reminders, which encourage me to do my daily practice. It also keeps a running total of consecutive days of practice, which as we've seen is a motivating factor. Your calendar can do this for you, but there are also meditation apps that incorporate tracking. Some people thrive on this kind of thing.

My language app's tracking gives me a reality check. Several times I've been convinced that I'd done my practice the previous day, but the app assures me I haven't. When there's a conflict between the app and my memory, I choose to believe the app, because I know that not only do I misremember things, but that I'll tend to do so in ways that are flattering to me.

Ultimately it's up to us to be honest with ourselves. Beware of any tendency to fudge your accounting, so that you consider yourself to have meditated when in reality you fell asleep two minutes into a late-night "beditation." And don't try to stretch the concept of "a day" beyond the breaking point by considering that the sit you did just after midnight counted for yesterday's sit, because it took place between waking and going back to sleep, but also for today's sit, because it took place during the current calendar day. When these temptations arise, take a deep breath and let go. Be honest with yourself about what's going on.

Sitting with others, or sharing your meditation track record with them, can help keep you motivated by keeping you accountable. You and a friend can check in with each other every day. You can even meditate together. For a long time I used to meditate daily with a friend in a video call, and it was helpful for us both. If you're unable to do something like that, you can at least check in with your meditation buddy by text message, email, or phone, and let each other know when you've meditated. You can also offer each other support, encouragement, and advice. This social connection can make your practice more enjoyable.

In recent years I've been meditating at the same time every morning with a group of other practitioners. It's a mainstay of my day. We're all grateful to each other just for showing up, because it's so motivating and supportive.

An online meditation community or forum is also an opportunity to share your practice with others. In my own Wildmind community, we sometimes do month-long "Get Your Sit Together" booster courses, and as part of these we share how many consecutive days we've meditated, continuing long beyond the initial twenty-eight-day period. The fact that we're making our successes and failures public is a powerful motivational factor. It's also good practice in being transparent. We don't judge each other's slip-ups. Instead, we offer encouragement and celebration.

Accountability Through Self-Blackmail

One final and rather radical form of motivation is self-blackmail. For example, you can make out a check to some cause that you despise, put it in a stamped, addressed envelope, and give it to a friend. The friend has instructions to mail the envelope if you don't reach some target you've set yourself, such as meditating every day for three months. To prevent your money being used in ways you disapprove of, you have to keep your friend apprised of your progress.

I've never used this form of accountability myself, but it's worked for enough people that whole websites have evolved for the purpose of self-blackmail. One of those is a site called "Go Fucking Do It" (gofuckingdoit.com) where you pay a penalty for not meeting your target. Another with a similar premise is Stickk (stickk.com), which was founded by professors from Yale. Many apps that leverage self-blackmail have come and gone over the years, but these two have proven sticking power. If they happen to have vanished by the time you read this, no doubt other websites will replace them, because for some people self-blackmail is effective as a motivational strategy.

Take a look right now at your social support and accountability system, and see what you can do to strengthen it. "I meditate every day. It's just what I do. It's part of who I am. I hold myself accountable."

Going Deeper

Our individuality is highly porous. We're open to having our opinions, actions, attitudes, and emotions affected by others. We know a lot about this because of a long-term medical project called the Framingham Heart Study. This began in 1952 as an attempt to pinpoint what factors helped or hindered cardiac health. It's because of the Framingham study that we learned that smoking is bad for your heart and exercise is good for it. Believe it or not, these things were not known, or were disputed, for a long time prior to the start of the study. Science rocks!

It's also because of the Framingham study that we know about the phenomenon of "social contagion," whereby habits and emotions spread through populations. If your friends happen to be overweight, you're more likely to put on the pounds yourself. If your friends smoke, you're more likely to become a slave to nicotine. If you have friends who exercise, you're more likely to do likewise.

Analysis over many years of the lives of tens of thousands of people and their hundreds of thousands of social connections reveal that there are clusters of happy and unhappy people within the Framingham population. It's not just that birds of a feather flock together—that miserable people seek out other miserable people, for example—but that emotional attitudes are catching. If you develop a friendship with someone who's happy, you'll become happier too, and so will your existing friends. And their friends will also experience a bump in their happiness levels, and so will *their* friend's friends. The effect of one happy person can be measured as far as three degrees of separation into the wider community.[19]

No one was doing this kind of quantitative study at the time of the Buddha, but he observed that who we spend time with influences us. If we associate with people who are unkind or untruthful, then their traits are apt to become ours by means of social osmosis. If we have friends who are compassionate and honest, the porosity of our selves means that we're inclined to develop the same attributes.

The Buddha talked about the friend who diverts us into unskillful behavior as being a *papamitta*, or bad friend, and the one who encourages what's best in us as a *kalyanamitta*, or a good, admirable, or spiritual friend. When his cousin and attendant, Ananda, remarked that these skillful friendships make up fully half of the spiritual life, the Buddha famously said that friendship is *the whole* of the spiritual life.

What did he mean by that? After all, my meditation practice is something that I essentially do on my own. Even if others are present, it's an internal activity, taking place in the confines of my own being. Or so it seems. But how did I learn to meditate? Back in the late 1970s I was taught the basics of two meditation techniques by a fellow Scotsman called Susiddhi, who's now sadly passed away. I refined what he taught me from what I learned on various retreats, by attending more meditation classes, and through reading books. Certainly, I applied myself creatively to my practice. I tested what he and others taught, and worked out for myself what worked and what didn't. Our rugged individualist culture would put the emphasis on the "I" in those sentences: *I* attended classes. *I* learned from books. But nothing would have happened were it not for the people who taught the classes, wrote the books, and so on. I would have had nothing to work with had they not taught me.

Even though my meditation practice takes place internally, I'm aware that it's supported by those around me. Early on, I realized that it was easier to sit through mental and physical discomfort if others were sitting still around me. On my own I was more fidgety and might sometimes cut my practice time short. The presence of others brought a sense of solidarity and stability. Having others around me to support my intention to practice gave me confidence and stillness. We are porous, and our practice is collective.

So if we want to meditate regularly, it's good to associate with others. It's especially good to associate with those who have a Rock-Solid Daily Meditation Practice. We can gain regularity from them by osmosis, and we can learn practical tips from them. This means it's worth creating the time to meditate collectively.

If we can sit with others, that's wonderful. But perhaps even more important is to share our progress, our struggles, and our successes and failures with them. This helps keep us accountable. It keeps us regular. It helps us become Rock-Solid Daily Meditators. And we are doing the same for them, too, because others too are porous and influenced osmotically. Over time we can develop relationships of great trust. We know that we can share our difficulties and our failures, and have them heard supportively and sympathetically, by those who have been through the same thing.

Reflection

Spend some time thinking about how you're affected by others—not just how they make you feel, but the skillful and unskillful qualities they have that rub off on you. Notice things like "Oh, I'm more cynical when I'm around such-and-such" or "Interesting! That person's calmness brings out the same quality in me." It's worth thinking about whether you can spend more time with people who bring out the best in you, and less with those who activate your less skillful side. Write something about this, so that it becomes more conscious and real for you.

Last Words

In the West, and particularly in the United States, there's a culture of rugged individuality that leads us to believe that anything of real significance has to be done without help. This works against the fact that genuine spiritual practice requires the positive influence of others. We need to learn to trust others so that we can increase our personal porosity and open ourselves up to those influences.

DAY 7

Chain Your Habits

Practice Reminder

Remember to sit for at least five minutes. *You meditate every day. It's just what you do. It's part of who you are.* You can do your practice now if you haven't already. Then celebrate to make yourself feel good. Finally, record your progress so that you have a visual reminder of your practice to inspire you to keep going.

Today

Let's look today at how you can integrate your meditation practice into your life.

Strategies

When do you meditate? Do you have a set time and place? Or are you fitting it in when you can? What reminds you to meditate? Do you set electronic reminders, or do you trust your memory?

Now, you don't need to set reminders to brush your teeth or shower; those things are just part of your routine. They follow on from other habitual actions, so that it's something like: wake up, go to the bathroom, have breakfast, shower, brush teeth, get dressed, go to work. No willpower or electronic reminders are needed. The ideal would be to have your sitting practice embedded in the matrix of your daily habits in just the same way: I've just done such-and-such; that means it's meditation time.

Your meditation practice shouldn't be an afterthought. It needs a home. Experts say that in establishing a new habit it's helpful to anchor it to an existing one. I've found this to be the case too. I used to keep forgetting to take my cholesterol medication, until I hit on putting a piece of tape on my toothbrush handle. After a while I no longer needed the tape: when I brush my teeth in the morning I automatically remember to take my tablet. I used to keep forgetting to fill my dogs' water bowl, then I got into the habit of filling it every morning and evening when I fed them.

Anchoring a new habit to an old one makes it much more likely that you'll remember to do it. Think of this as creating a chain of habits, with each action being like an individual link. If you normally have a cup of coffee first thing after getting up in the morning, you might chain your meditation habit to that habit. Your coffee-drinking can become a ritual preparation for meditating, or it can be a reward that you give yourself afterward. I'm more of a reward guy myself, but that's just me. Either way can work.

Before I learned how to meditate every day, my chain was something like this:

- Wake up.
- Pick up my phone and get lost in reading emails, social media, and news.
- Realize it was late and get out of bed.
- Make and eat breakfast.
- Shower and shave.
- If there was time, have a very short sit.
- Go to work disappointed that I'd spent my time poorly.

Meditation was the geeky kid who was always last to be picked for the high school soccer game.

For me, the biggest factor in creating a better chain of habits was to avoid opening my phone first thing in the morning (see Day 3: Master the Hindrance in Your Pocket). After I had cut my phone from my morning routine, it looked like this:

- Wake up.
- Get out of bed.
- Have a refreshing glass of orange juice.
- Meditate for thirty or forty minutes.
- Have breakfast (and maybe check my notifications on my phone).
- Shower and shave.
- Head to work with a glowing sense that my day has started well.

Wake, rise, OJ, and sit became my routine. This sequence became the chain of habits that anchored my sitting and gave it a home. And the most important link having been given pride of place, the following habits in my chain were now infused with a sense of peace because I'd done what needed to be done. In response to changing circumstances my morning routine has been reorganized a few times since then, but my meditation practice is still the most important thing in my chain of habits. Everything stops for sitting.

See what you can anchor your meditation practice to. Your practice needs a definite trigger. For me the taste of my morning OJ became a signal: "Time to sit!" For you it might simply be getting out of bed. It might be the taste of coffee. It might be the thought of coffee afterward. Or maybe the early morning isn't practical for you. Maybe it's lunchtime that will be the trigger for your daily sit. Maybe it's coming home from work and having a shower. Maybe it's bedtime. But you need an anchor. Without one, your meditation habit is unmoored, untethered. It doesn't have a true place in your life, it doesn't have a home, and at some point you'll find you forget to do it.

"I meditate every day. It's just what I do. It's part of who I am. I give my practice a special place in my life."

Going Deeper

What happens once the time you've set aside for your meditation practice is over? Do you open your eyes gently, slowly ease your body out of its meditation posture, and start moving about in the world mindfully? Do you cherish the mindfulness and kindness that have arisen in your meditation practice and let them guide you gracefully into your next activity? Or do you shove them aside in your haste to get on to the next thing? Unfortunately, the latter is very common.

When I'm leading retreats or workshops and end a meditation session with a bell, some people virtually explode out of their meditation postures the moment they hear wood touch brass. To counter this, I encourage people to regard the sound of the bell as a meditation in its own right. We can listen moment by moment, attentive to the shimmering vibrations in the air as they become softer and softer until they fade away into stillness. We can keep listening until we're no longer sure we're hearing bell or silence, and then continue to listen to the silence, letting that too be a meditation practice.

We can allow our attention to connect gradually with other sensations arising from the outside world—the light surrounding us and coming through our closed eyelids, the sense of space around us, the sounds that fill that space—and the physical contact the body is making with the outside world, including our butt on its seat, our feet on the floor, and the air resting on our skin. We can *ease* our awareness back into the outside world, bringing with us the stillness, mindfulness, and kindness we've connected with as we sat.

Years ago when I was leading guided meditations I'd talk about "bringing the practice to a close." I no longer do that, and instead my last words are about "bringing our attention and our practice more fully into the world." I want to avoid giving the impression that once we open our eyes the qualities we've been cultivating will just fade away and be lost—or worse, be crudely dropped as if we're finished with them. Instead, those qualities become part of the way we relate to the world around us. There is no end to practice. Practice goes on.

We tend to use the terms *practice* and *meditation* interchangeably, but it's more helpful if we regard the whole of our lives as practice, as a conscious attempt to cultivate the spiritual qualities that improve our own lives and the lives of others. Everything we do can be done mindfully and with kindness.

Not long before he died, the Buddha exhorted his followers to live with mindfulness (*sati*) and intentionality (*sampajañña*). He described mindful living in terms of observing one's body, feelings, and mind, and how all three of these work together—either to our detriment or benefit. He described living with intentionality in terms of monitoring our daily activities:

> *How does a spiritual practitioner cultivate intentionality? It's when they act intentionally when going out and coming back; when looking ahead and aside; when bending and extending the limbs; when bearing the outer robe, bowl, and robes; when eating, drinking, chewing, and tasting; when urinating and defecating; when walking, standing, sitting, sleeping, waking, speaking, and keeping silent.*[20]

Intentionality, you might remember from Day 2, involves comparing what we're doing with our spiritual purpose. We're not simply going through life noticing the sensations that arise, but are also bearing in mind that we want to be calmer, kinder, happier, and at peace. With that aim in mind, we make sure that our actions support and lead us toward those goals.

This is the real meaning of ethics in Buddhist practice. It's not about following rules, obeying commandments, being a good Buddhist, or looking virtuous. It's about bringing more *intentionality* into our lives. The five precepts—not harming, not taking things that aren't ours, not misusing our sex lives, not lying, and not distorting our awareness through intoxication—are all guidelines we can use. They are the aims we bear in mind as we go through life. We can keep coming back to questions like, *Is what I'm about to do likely to hurt anyone? Is what I'm doing now? Am I being selfish to the detriment of others? Is what I'm saying really true?* and so on.

The five precepts are framed negatively, in terms of actions we undertake to avoid doing, but at various times the Buddha made it clear that they were to be accompanied by our cultivating the positive qualities that are their complements. We read that a spiritual practitioner reflects on the first precept as both an abstention from causing harm and a positive quality of compassion:

> As long as they live, the perfected ones give up killing living creatures, renouncing the rod and the sword. They are scrupulous and kind, and live full of compassion for all living beings.[21]

Taking the behavior of the enlightened ones as our model of a good life, we can resolve to live with the same spirit of compassion as they do. And this is a reminder that the deeper purpose of practice is to make our entire lives an expression of the kind of wisdom and compassion that the Buddha himself embodied. Our entire life becomes practice.

Reflection

Write down a list of qualities that you want to bring into your day-to-day life. Make notes of how specifically you could embody them. For example, if I identify that I aspire to be kinder, I can resolve to call a friend I haven't seen in a while to see how they're getting on, make a point of expressing appreciation to my partner, or to let other drivers merge in traffic. These things become personal precepts that guide my actions.

Last Words

Bear in mind how you would ideally like to live and, as best you can, treat every moment as an opportunity to move toward that ideal. For example, you can treat every moment in life as an opportunity to move toward being calmer, more present, and more compassionate.

DAY 8

Celebrate the Small Stuff

Practice Reminder

Sit, if you haven't done so already. Perhaps by now you feel like you'd like to sit for longer than five minutes. Allow yourself to do that, if possible. Remember to celebrate that you've meditated. And afterward, create a visual reminder of your success—grow your chain!

Today

Now, let's look at how you can incorporate moments of celebration into your meditation practice itself, bringing more joy into your sitting.

Strategies

I've been encouraging you to celebrate after you've meditated. But you can also bring moments of celebration into your meditation practice itself. Because celebrating gives rise to pleasure, it makes our meditation practice more enjoyable. And if your practice is more enjoyable then you'll want to do it more. Once again, we're back to the rewards component of habit formation.

One of the things that can make our meditation practice frustrating is that the mind wanders a lot. We can learn to accept that that happens, but it's still no fun. So what I suggest is that you consciously celebrate the return to mindfulness that happens when your attention emerges from a period of distraction.

It works like this. You have the usual cycle:

1. Get distracted.
2. Realize you've been distracted.
3. Return to the focus of the meditation practice.
4. Get distracted again.
5. Rinse and repeat.

I'm sure you have been given the excellent advice that when you realize the mind has been wandering it's best not to judge yourself. What I suggest you add to that suggestion is that in that moment you celebrate and be grateful that mindfulness has reestablished itself. As you return to the practice, you can simply say to yourself, "Yes!" or "Yay!" Notice any pleasant feelings that arise when you do this. Don't try to intensify these feelings or do anything with them. Just let them be and observe them as you continue to breathe in and out.

Now the cycle looks like this:

1. Get distracted.
2. Realize your mind has come back to mindful awareness.
3. Celebrate that fact as you return to the focus of the meditation practice.
4. Feel good until you get distracted again.
5. Rinse and repeat.

This way we bring more pleasure into the practice.

Notice the shift in focus from realizing we've been distracted to realizing that your mind has come back to mindful awareness. It's the same thing described in a different way, but this second perspective is affirming. It recognizes that our attention has stepped out of distracted thinking and into mindfulness. This is a significant—and even miraculous—event. It's something you can be grateful for when it happens.

You can also be grateful that the return of mindful awareness happens *all on its own*. You didn't have to do anything. You don't decide to return to mindfulness. It just happens. In fact, for every time that the mind loses mindfulness, there is a time that it finds its way back there again. The mind always finds its own way home. This is an extraordinary thing that we often just fail to see. But once we've realized this is indeed the case, we can celebrate it: *I'm mindful again! Yay! I didn't even have to make it happen! Yay!*

Just as celebrating at the end of a period of meditation provides a reward, making it more likely that we'll be drawn to meditation in the future, when we celebrate coming home to mindfulness we make being present more appealing. We create an incentive for mindfulness to arise.

It's important that the celebration be brief. You don't want to turn it into another distraction, for example by saying "Yay!" and then following that up with a bunch of other thoughts, like "I'm really getting good at meditation. Maybe I'll never get distracted ever again. Oh, this feels so good. It's better than chocolate . . ." and so on. That's obviously not helpful. Just give yourself a micro-boost of appreciation and celebration, enjoy any pleasure that results, and continue with the practice. The pleasure is a reward that will make you want to come back for more.

"I meditate every day. It's just what I do. It's part of who I am. And I choose to celebrate every return to mindfulness."

Going Deeper

Our minds have what psychologists call a "negativity bias." If you think back on your earliest memories, there's a good chance that a lot of them are about unpleasant events—maybe of getting lost in a store or of being humiliated. My own earliest memories are from the age of two, in which I remember, among other things, throwing up after my dad gave me a sip of his beer and my hair catching fire when I climbed onto a stool to watch an egg boiling on our gas stove. The more enjoyable things have slipped away.

There's an evolutionary reason for this negativity bias in our memories. Early primates that didn't vividly remember threats to their well-being took more risks and removed themselves from the gene pool. You and I are the descendants of the jumpy, pessimistic primates that survived long enough to reproduce. When I think of the early memories I mentioned, they're exactly the kinds of things that would have been important to our forebears' survival. The primate equivalent of my unhappy childhood beer-drinking adventure would have been something like, "I ate that new fruit and it made me sick." And our hominin forebears needed to have a clear understanding of the dangers of fire. Vivid memories of such things are powerful motivators.

Negativity bias involves not just our memories, but our current perceptions. If someone is polite to you many times, but then is rude to you just once, you're likely to think of that person as rude rather than as polite, even though the predominance of their behavior is the other way around. Studies show that if we are asked to look at a mixture of positive and negative images, we spend more time looking at the negative ones. Studies of intimate relationships show that for them to be successful there has to be a ratio of five positive interactions (being helpful, offering a genuine compliment) for every negative one (being snarky, ignoring your partner). Our brains are wired to give priority to negative perceptions, and we have to work hard at being positive to redress that imbalance.

The Buddha was aware of the relative rarity of positive emotions when he said that a person who is grateful and thankful is a rare thing in this world.[22] He encouraged the conscious cultivation of appreciation, first asking his companions if they had heard an old jackal howling at the crack of dawn, and then pointing out that there was more gratitude and appreciation in that miserable animal than there was in some of his followers. He said, "You should train like this: 'We will be grateful and thankful. We won't forget even a small thing done for us.'"[23] He's suggesting that we consciously cultivate appreciation so that we can overcome the mind's tendency to seek out and remember the negative.

Consciously seeking things to appreciate is another way of bringing practice into our daily life. Part of the mind's negativity bias is that once we have a good thing, we tend to take it for granted rather feel appreciative toward it. For example, you almost certainly have hot and cold running water in your house, and probably you don't think at all about how wonderful that is. If you have any feelings at all about this, they may involve mild frustration about how long you have to wait for the hot water to come through the pipes, or for the cold water to get really cold. It's only when things go wrong that we begin to appreciate how wonderful it is to have running water.

Imagining life without our modern conveniences is a good way of triggering gratitude. I've been to places in the world where people have to fetch water from a communal supply and carry it home in buckets. Just remembering that makes me appreciative. In many parts of the world, people don't have electricity in their homes—or if they do it's unreliable and goes out for hours at a time. My grandmother didn't have a bathroom in her house and had to use a communal toilet. (Remembering that makes me grateful indeed!) Can you imagine life without sewers? Roads? A walk through a Victorian-era graveyard shows us evidence of a shocking number of child deaths, which were accepted as the norm. Now, infant mortality is rare. Despite our seeming to be surrounded by news of violent crime and wars, our lives are incredibly safe. Examinations of skeletons from ten thousand years ago suggest that those people had a one in seven chance of dying violently. Nowadays, dying violently is so rare that most of us expect to die of old age, or of the cancers or heart problems that result simply from living for a long time. Thinking of what life used to be like—and still is for people in many parts of the world—helps me be more appreciative.

You don't have to consider the absence of things you take for granted if you want to be appreciative. Try just looking around you and find things that you enjoy. Right now I can enjoy and appreciate the oil painting I was given by a friend, the color my partner and I picked for our walls, the brass midcentury wall decoration that my partner found in a yard sale, the lampshade the previous owners of this house left behind, the curtains that shut out the world when we want privacy, and many other things. When I take the time to notice and appreciate the good things in my life in this way, my mood shifts. I feel buoyed up. I feel happy. I feel blessed.

This is something we can all do. Give it a go and see how you get on.

Reflection

Spend time reflecting on the many benefits around you that make your life easier. As you call each to mind, say the words "Thank you," either out loud or in your mind. Notice what effect this has on how you feel.

Last Words

If you take the time to appreciate the many blessings in your life, you'll feel happier. This is a simple thing you can do to bring your spiritual practice into your daily life, and it's deeply transformative.

DAY 9

Make Practice Enjoyable at the Beginning, Middle, and End

Practice Reminder

The most important thing is to sit. It's just what you do. It's part of who you are. Celebrate having practiced, so that you feel good about it. Also, remember to record your practice, and enjoy seeing the chain of days grow longer.

Today

Let's look at things we can do that bring more of a sense of joy into our meditation practice.

Strategies

When people find it easy to do something like running or meditating, it's because they have found ways to make it enjoyable, so that the habit has become rewarding. Here are some suggestions, including a few things I've presented before, for ways to make your practice richer and more satisfying:

- Make the place you meditate pleasing. Keep it clean and tidy, and decorate it nicely.

- Bring a little ritual into your meditation, perhaps by lighting some candles and incense. These activities can be comforting and inspiring, and the scent and the flickering light add a pleasing sensory accompaniment to your practice. Chanting before and after meditation can also be enjoyable. (We'll discuss ritual further on Day 14.) Wrap yourself in a cozy blanket if it's not too warm to do so.
- Often it helps to listen to a guided meditation. Doing this, you're less likely to feel you're on your own. If the guidance is done well, then you'll feel like you don't have to do so much work. You may also learn new skills, which makes the practice more interesting and enjoyable. And if you choose a meditation where the instructor's voice is easy on the ears, this too adds to the pleasure of sitting.
- Find things to be appreciative of, from being protected from the elements to the ability to make choices.
- See this moment as precious. The very existence of awareness is miraculous.
- Sit with soft eyes, letting the muscles around the eyes be at rest, and letting the focus within your eyes be gentle. (If you're not familiar with this approach to meditation, try Meditation 3 from the recordings that complement this book.) This helps bring a sense of ease into your experience.
- Be kind. First, remember what it feels like to look with love. Next, let that memory trigger a kind, appreciative inner gaze, so that you meet every experience with warmth.
- Let there be a little playfulness in the way you relate to yourself. When you find yourself taking things seriously, be prepared to have a little laugh at your own expense—fondly, of course.
- When things don't go according to plan—for example, if you find yourself very tired or your mind is more distractable than

usual—practice acceptance. Say to yourself, "This is just how things are right now." Release yourself from the obligation to be perfect.

- Celebrate every time you recognize that your mind has come home to mindful awareness.
- Celebrate having meditated, preferably with expansive physical gestures, such as raising your arms over your head.
- Enjoy seeing your chain of daily meditations grow longer. This is one reason it's good to use a paper calendar to show how you're meditating, day after day after day. Treat this as a friendly competition with yourself.
- Remember that when you meditate you're doing a good thing for yourself that also helps others. It's rare that people consciously work on themselves in this way. Hold in your heart an awareness of the preciousness of your practice until you feel an emotional response to its goodness.

Some of these strategies, such as the prospect of returning to a favorite guided meditation or anticipating your chain growing, bring pleasurable anticipation. Others, like being kind and playful, bring more enjoyment into the practice itself. And celebrating can bring pleasure at the end of a period of practice. Tapping into many strategies, our practice can feel good at the beginning, middle, and end.

"I meditate every day. It's just what I do. It's part of who I am. I choose to make my practice enjoyable."

Going Deeper

On the way to enlightenment, the Buddha-to-be spent years avoiding pleasure and exposing himself to discomfort. Along with many other people at that time, he practiced austerities, or *tapas*. This word has nothing to do with tasty snacks in a Spanish bar. It literally means "heat," probably because a common form of ascetic practice involved meditating under the hot noon-day sun, sometimes also surrounded—just to make things even more hardcore—by four fires.

This kind of thing may seem weird to us now, but back then it was all the rage among a certain set of spiritual seekers. They understood pleasure and happiness to be inextricably bound up with the weaknesses of the flesh. They believed that to find liberation the mind had to completely master the body by denying it pleasure and accustoming it to pain and discomfort. Gotama bought into this for a while and did things like holding his breath until he was racked with pain, hauling out his hair and beard by the roots, sleeping on a bed of thorns, and starving himself with extreme fasting. According to his own account he got nothing much out of all this except for bringing himself close to death through starvation.

After he'd realized the futility of these *tapas* practices, Gotama began to reflect on what he might try next. The answer came to him in the form of an old memory. As a child he'd been sitting under the shade of a tree, watching his father plow a field, and he'd slipped into a natural meditative state of calm, alert joyfulness. Looking back now, he realized that although he'd spent his adult life afraid of the pleasure that can arise in meditation, that pleasure can in fact be completely wholesome. He asked himself,

> *"Why am I afraid of that pleasure, for it has nothing to do with sensual pleasures or unskillful qualities?" Then I thought, "I'm not afraid of that pleasure, for it has nothing to do with sensual pleasures or unskillful qualities."*[24]

It struck him that there was something powerful about this state of easeful, nongrasping happiness. In fact, he wondered, "Might this be the path to the spiritual awakening?" and his intuition responded in no uncertain terms, "Yes, this *is* the path to awakening!" He'd found an approach to enlightenment that involved being deeply at ease with yourself, physically and mentally, letting peace and joy arise naturally. This approach was radically different from the notion that you could find awakening through intense willpower.

Although I said that the ascetic practices of ancient India might strike us as weird, there's something of the spirit of the ascetic practices of the Buddha's time in our modern habits of working long hours, feeling guilty about having downtime, and depriving ourselves of sleep so that we can be more productive. Like the ancient ascetics, many of us today believe that a long-term goal (enlightenment in one case, and "success" in the other) can be achieved by accustoming ourselves to pain and self-denial in the present moment. Now, it's true that in order to gain future rewards we sometimes need to do things now that are challenging and uncomfortable. Learning to delay gratification is an essential part of becoming a mature human being. But sometimes we're simply misguided, and we live a life that's all delay, all self-denial, and no gratification. The future ease and happiness that was supposed to follow always stays just ahead of us and never actually arrives. We can get used to living like this. It's not quite the same thing as meditating naked under the noonday Indian sun, surrounded by four fires, but it's along the same lines.

Now, if you know about early Buddhism, you might be aware that although the Buddha was against asceticism, he and his monastic disciples lived mainly by eating other people's left-over food, dressed in robes made from rags, wouldn't listen to music, slept under trees, and owned nothing but their robes and begging bowls. So what's that about?

The way of life of early Buddhist monastics was certainly austere. They didn't live in organized monasteries at that time—that was a development that came after the Buddha's time—and as I've described they lived very simply. The point of such radical simplicity, however, was not self-punishment. They kept life simple so that they could focus on spiritual practice. They weren't afraid of pleasure or happiness as such, just the pleasure and happiness that came from sensual attractions that would complicate life and take them away from a life of full-time mindfulness and meditation.

The Buddha, remember, had come to the realization that he didn't need to be afraid of pleasure and joy because there were forms of pleasure and joy that were skillful. The pleasure and joy that come from meditation are, as he recognized, "the path to awakening," because they are the felt experience of us being completely at ease with ourselves, having resolved all inner conflict.

In my own life I've been at my most happy when I've been on retreat, living a life of extreme simplicity, with long periods of silence, few responsibilities, lots of time to walk silently in nature, and (best of all) lots of meditation. What a contrast that is from the stressful business of providing a taxi service for my children, paying bills, picking up dog poop, working full-time, and maintaining my house and its yard.

The austere life that the early monastic community lived had its challenges. Many monks and nuns missed family life and sexual activity, and this was one of the main reasons that people disrobed, but for many others it was a deeply joyful way of living—calm, and full of love and companionship. They were doing something deeply meaningful. Meditation was an important part of all this.

Although meditation is meant to be enjoyable, a lot of contemporary meditators don't experience it that way. So it's worth asking ourselves whether we're unconsciously bringing elements of asceticism into our meditation. Do we regard it as work—in the sense of a task done dutifully, where its lack of pleasure proves its worthiness? Do we regard it as one of those things that's not joyful but will *somehow* (maybe, sometime) lead to joy arising in the future?

If we wonder at all about the lack of pleasure in our meditation, we may think that some sort of advanced meditation technique might be needed for our sitting practice to be enjoyable, or that perhaps we need some kind of psychotherapeutic breakthrough. Yet in most cases all we need to do is to let ourselves relax a little and stop taking ourselves so seriously. A question I often ask myself is, "Is there anything I'm doing right now that's suppressing joy?" In the wake of that question I might notice tension in the body, and let it soften. I might notice a seriousness in my attitude because I'm striving after results, and let go. And as soon as I let go, joy arises. It's as if it's always been there, waiting for me to relax enough to notice it. And it's wonderful that joy is so easily found, because when meditation is joyful we find ourselves wanting to return to it again and again.

Reflection

Ask yourself at random moments, "Is there anything I'm doing right now that's suppressing joy?" Observe anything you do that is inhibiting a sense of ease. Note what happens when you let go of those things, and make a note of all this in your journal.

Last Words

There is a wholesome joy that comes from practice—from being loving, appreciative, and mindful of the small things in life. This joy is not to be feared, and if it's not present at least some of the time, it may be that we've taken on board the unhelpful idea that life is meant to be unpleasant.

DAY 10

Consider Every Sit a Good Sit

Practice Reminder

Sit. Celebrate. Record your progress.

Today

Our tendency to regard only meditations that are unusually calm or joyful as good sits is unhelpful. Try regarding every sit you do as a good sit and as worthy of celebration, simply because it happened.

Strategies

When a friend wrote to tell me about a good meditation he'd had, contrasting it with his usual "bad" meditations, I reflected—not for the first time—on how the whole notion of "good" and "bad" meditations is flawed and unhelpful. My friend's "good" meditation was one in which his mind was unusually calm. Sure, you have some sits that are much more pleasant and enjoyable than others, and it's natural to get excited about this. But if you regard this as a "good" meditation, then by implication the rest of them are "bad," or at least unworthy of our appreciation. And so by defaulting into that particular definition of "good" meditations, we make most of our other meditation experiences seem substandard. That's not helpful, because we're dissing the work we're doing.

Because I hadn't slept well, my own meditation that morning was mostly dreamy, with lots of distracted thinking. I may even have fallen asleep at times. But I felt pleased about it simply because I did it. Was that a "good" meditation? Not in most people's estimation, nor when weighed against my average experience. But does that matter? No! The meditation was what it was, and how I feel about it doesn't make any difference to that fact, except that if I regard any sit I do as a good sit, I'm free to feel good about doing it. If I categorize my meditations into "good," "bad," and "meh" I'm reducing my opportunities to feel happy about having done something good.

I choose to be pleased at the very fact of having done my daily practice. I bring this about by celebrating every sit. ("Yay, me!") The pleasant feeling that comes from celebrating helps keep me practicing daily. If you want to keep meditating regularly as well, celebrate the fact of meditating. Every meditation you do is a "good meditation." Having been tired or distracted needn't stop you from being pleased that you showed up and meditated.

You might want to bear in mind two things. The first is, "Any meditation you can walk away from is a good meditation." The fact you meditate is more important than the exact amount of calmness or joy you had. The other is, "The only bad sits are the ones you didn't do." If you're sitting, it's a good sit.

Naturally, if your mind becomes concentrated during a sit, or when joy or love arise, then you can be pleased by those occurrences as well. But they're a bonus, since you've already decided to feel pleased about the very fact of sitting.

Every sit is a good sit. Just keep going.

"I meditate every day. It's just what I do. It's part of who I am. The only bad sits are the ones I don't do."

Going Deeper

We often hear that mindfulness is nonjudgmental. This is true. Sometimes we hear that mindfulness is the whole of the spiritual path, and that it contains curiousity, wisdom, kindness, and compassion. This is not correct, and it's important to recognize this, because we can come to think that if mindfulness is nonjudgmental and mindfulness is the whole spiritual path, then spiritual practice must therefore be free of judgment, which it is not.

First, mindfulness is observation, and observation is free of judgment. So mindfulness is indeed nonjudgmental. But mindfulness is not the whole of the spiritual path, and spiritual practice intrinsically involves making judgments. Traditionally, mindfulness is just one part of a system of practice. It's just one factor in the eightfold path, for example, surrounded by other factors that it interacts with. Here, for context, is the whole list, with some brief explanations:

1. Right view: cultivating wisdom, including knowing what is and isn't skillful
2. Right intention: cultivating skillful emotions, such as faith, kindness, and compassion
3. Right speech: communicating truthfully, kindly, helpfully, and in ways that promote harmony
4. Right action: conducting yourself ethically in the world
5. Right livelihood: ensuring your work is an expression of your practice
6. Right effort: eradicating unskillful thoughts and emotions, while cultivating the skillful
7. Right mindfulness: observing what's going on, so that the other factors of the path know what they're working with

8. Right concentration: developing all the forgoing skillful qualities through meditative absorption

Here it's obvious that mindfulness is just part of our spiritual practice. Mindfulness is *seeing*. It's *observing*. It isn't inherently kind; kindness is part of the practice of right intention. Mindfulness isn't inherently wise; wisdom is right view. Mindfulness doesn't itself take action; it just observes. But it is a catalytic quality. Mindfulness makes it possible for us to mobilize the other factors of the eightfold path, because it shows us what's going on. And unless we know what's going on, we can't know how we should act.

Notice how, in the eightfold path, each of the factors is prefixed with the word "right," which is *samma* in Pali. Each "right" factor has a corresponding "wrong" factor, the word wrong being *micchā* in Pali. To a large extent, spiritual practice is about exercising judgments about what's helpful and unhelpful in terms of living well, and on the basis of that, making choices.

Mindfulness, discriminative awareness (or wisdom), and action work together, as illustrated in one of the Buddha's discourses.

> *They make an effort to give up wrong view and embrace right view: that's their right effort. Mindfully they give up wrong view and take up right view: that's their right mindfulness. So these three things keep running and circling around right view, namely: right view, right effort, and right mindfulness.*[25]

In a note on the translation of this discourse, Bhikkhu Sujato remarks that "Right view understands what to do; right effort does the work; and right mindfulness monitors and checks."

If we didn't know what was going on within us, we wouldn't be able to take appropriate action. We would simply stumble through life, creating suffering for ourselves and others. And that, in fact, is what often happens, because we're more often unmindful than we are mindful. Once we've become mindfully aware of what's going on within us, we have choices about how to act. For example, we might observe that a thought has arisen, that the thought is angry, and that this anger is painful. That's mindfulness. There is no judgment here—no condemnation or approval. We're simply observing, seeing what's going on. Yet having observed that, other spiritual qualities can mobilize themselves. Right view reveals that the consequences of indulging in that angry thought will bring further pain and conflict in the future. Right effort finds glimmerings of patience and kindness and encourages them to shine forth. Right speech and action manifest that kindness in our words and in what we do. And so on.

Once when I was teaching a class on the eightfold path, someone who was there for the first time said that talking about "right" this and "wrong" that sounded judgmental. They'd expected the Buddha's teachings to be free of judgment. Yet we use the word *judgment* in different ways, depending on what the basis is for making judgments. To be judgmental means to categorize things into good and bad depending on how we feel about them. So if we get distracted in meditation we might categorize it as bad, and since we're the one who's getting distracted, we might also classify ourselves as a bad meditator or even as a bad person. This is all based on likes and dislikes.

The kind of judgment the Buddha is advocating in distinguishing right view from wrong view, and so on, is simply to do with the consequences of each of those things. Wrong views, intentions, speech and so on tend to cause suffering, which is not what we ultimately want in life. Right views, intentions, and speech tend to help free us from suffering, which is something we ultimately aspire to.

So there's judgment involved in all spiritual practice. We distinguish between those things that are helpful for our well-being and those that are unhelpful. In essence this is a kind of judgment. But it's not judgmental, because it's simply based on an awareness of the felt consequences of the various choices we can make in life. Perhaps we need to think of what we're doing as "nonjudgmental judgment."

Reflection

Having read the brief description and examples of the eightfold path above, can you look at your experience and write a few words about how the factors of the path work together in your practice?

Last Words

As far as possible, mindfulness should always be practiced accompanied by a wise awareness of whether we're acting skillfully or unskillfully, and wise actions that help free us and others from suffering.

DAY 11

Step It Up

Practice Reminder

If possible, try meditating for a little longer today, even if it's just by a minute or two. Or see if you can do a second meditation, even if it's just a brief one. Remember to celebrate! And track your progress!

Today

Today we'll look at the desirability of making your sits longer, how this can be challenging for some people, and what we can do that helps with that challenge.

Strategies

If you're following this program you've committed to sitting every day for at least five minutes. Five minutes isn't a lot of time to spend in meditation, and you probably already wonder if it's enough to make a difference in your life. It's hard to say: One study showed that thirteen minutes of meditation a day improved people's mood and attention, but only if they did it for eight weeks.[26] Another study showed that just ten minutes of meditation a day was helpful.[27] It's possible that five minutes daily is just not long enough to make a significant difference to how you feel in the long term, even if you feel a bit happier and more relaxed after a sit.

However, I don't suggest committing to a baseline of five minutes of meditation a day because it's enough to trigger an experience of awakening or even radically change your emotional states. I suggest five minutes because it's doable, and so it allows us to create the habit of daily meditation. It's a foot in the door. Once you've started to meditate daily you feel much better about yourself. Feeling more confident can bring about all kinds of changes in your life. You might realize, if you're capable of this, what else might you be able to do?

With your five-minute daily micro-habit established, and with some newfound confidence under your belt, you can step it up and meditate for a bit longer each day. If you're used to meditating for just five minutes, you might find it hard to jump to longer periods of practice. Guided meditations are helpful here. With a guided meditation you have someone talking you through the experience. They may be offering suggestions that make the practice more enjoyable. It may even be so enjoyable that the time flies. *Whoa! Was that fifteen minutes already!* So, I'd recommend using guided meditations when you're stepping up your practice.

Don't be overly ambitious, though. One common reason people fail to keep up a daily practice is because they aim too high. If you're used to five-minute sits, then ten minutes may already be a challenge, and to jump straight to twenty minutes might be setting yourself up for failure. If you're an experienced meditator, though, and often do longer sits on retreat or at a meditation group or class, you're in a different situation. Doing longer sits might not be a problem. But sustaining them every day might be. So remember that you always have the option to meditate for only five minutes. There will be days when that's all you can manage, and five minutes is fine.

An alternative to making your sits longer is to do more of them. Sitting twice a day for five minutes might be a good option for you.

"I meditate every day. It's just what I do. It's part of who I am. I practice while sensitive to my needs."

Going Deeper

Longer sits can give the mind more time to settle, so that the mind can become calm. But sometimes we find that it's hard to sit for longer than we're used to. Physical discomfort can become a challenge when we extend the length of our sits, but our emotions can be the larger problem. The restless parts of the mind might declare, "Wait! We had an agreement! I agreed to quiet down for *five* minutes. And now you're meditating for *ten*? You're in breach of our agreement, you scoundrel! I object!" Even if you're adding a mere two or three minutes of extra time, you might develop a powerful urge to get off the cushion and go do something else instead. Your body also might have something to say about sitting longer. It takes a while for your knees, your butt, and so on to get used to more protracted meditations. But you will get used to it, both mentally and physically. The body and mind recalibrate how long they consider "normal" for meditating.

We can only really gain confidence in our ability to sit for longer by actually sitting for longer, which means that the pain that comes from extending the amount of time we sit for is inevitable. You're just going to have to work through it. No pain, no gain.

In fact this discomfort is a valuable arena for cultivating equanimity, which is an attitude of mental balance arising from acceptance. To strengthen your equanimity, first, notice the mental resistance that manifests as thoughts such as "This is awful. I can't stand it." Recognize that these thoughts are normal. They're not a sign of failure. You don't have to push these thoughts away, or to make them stop. But neither do you need to believe them and indulge them. You can simply contain and observe them. To contain feelings of discomfort it helps to let the eyes be soft, restful, and almost unfocused. This helps to create a sense of spaciousness in our awareness, so that instead of our inner gaze acting like a flashlight that picks out and accentuates our restless feelings, our inner field of attention is more like a lamp that illuminates many things. With our attention like a flashlight, which is our default mode of experiencing things, our discomfort is virtually the only thing we notice. Yet with our attention like a lamp, our uncomfortable feelings are just one small, although significant, part of our experience. Because they're no longer highlighted, they become easier to contain, and we're less likely to react to them.

With our restlessness perceived as just part of our experience, we can observe it as if from the outside, rather than, as it were, from within, which is the usual way we perceive discomfort. We can marshal our curiosity and notice where the discomfort is located in the body, what shape it has, what sensations it's made up of (pressure, tingling, movement, weight, and so on), and whether it's changing with the in breath and the out breath. We can recognize our discomfort to be just a sensation, like any other.

These two things—having a spacious awareness and being curious—allow us to be more at peace with discomfort. We can learn to simply be with it, no longer seeing it as an emergency we have to deal with, and instead accepting it. The mind is poised, balanced, not shaken by pleasure or pain. This is equanimity. Or at least it's what we're working toward. All this takes practice.

There are other very basic things that can help you get used to sitting for longer. Practicing with other people is one of them. Being with others who are sitting still gives us permission to be still, too. Seeing others sitting, apparently confidently, helps us to have confidence. The presence of others has a soothing, stabilizing effect on your mind. And once you've realized you can do a longer sit with others, you'll begin to develop the confidence that you can do it on your own, too. Also, if you get so restless that you want to get up and leave, you probably won't. The restlessness will still be there, but it'll be easier to ride it out.

It's especially useful to go to retreats or workshops that offer opportunities to do more intensive practice. These events might last just a couple of hours, a day, a weekend, or perhaps a week or more. Repeatedly doing substantial-length sits can blow away our self-imposed, imagined limitations as if they were never there. If you sit for an hour on retreat, then thirty minutes at home is a breeze, and the memory that ten minutes once seemed like an endurance test seems quaint.

In many practice traditions, periods of sitting are interspersed with walking meditations, and this pattern offers us another way of extending the length of our periods of practice. If you find it physically or emotionally challenging to meditate for long, you can start with a sit, transition to a walking meditation, and then end with another sit. In this way a thirty-minute period of practice needn't require sits that are longer than ten minutes or so. Standing meditation is another perfectly good alternative to walking meditation. You can find guided versions of both these practices among the recordings accompanying this book.

You can also mentally divide up a longer time into shorter sits. If you want to move from doing ten-minute meditations to sits that last for twenty minutes, then you can set a timer for the midway point. When the bell goes off, let your mind rest for a few breaths, and regard what you do after that as a "new" meditation.

By being strategic, we can change the mind's expectations, training ourselves to sit for longer, and bringing more depth to our practice.

Reflection

Have you previously overcome fears about sitting longer—for example when you've been on retreat? Reflect on what the process of working through those challenges was like. If this is not a process you've been through, try writing a journal entry as if you had. Write about the challenge of sitting for longer, and what strategies you would employ to get through the emotional discomfort. This can act as a rehearsal for when you do take this step.

Last Words

The challenge of learning to sit for longer gives us the opportunity to work through the discomfort of change. It gives us an opportunity to develop equanimity, or the ability to be present with our feelings without reacting to them. It gives us the opportunity to develop more faith in ourselves. Challenge is an opportunity for growth.

DAY 12

View Challenges and Setbacks as Opportunities

Practice Reminder

Keep coming back to our mantra: "I meditate every day. It's just what I do. It's part of who I am." It helps give rise to the spiritual quality of diligence (*appamāda*), which the Buddha regarded as the support for all other skillful qualities. Diligence is what keeps us going. Keep celebrating. Keep tracking how many consecutive days you've sat for.

Today

Sometimes our normal schedule is completely upended—for example, when we go on vacation or when we have to cope with an emergency, and even our plan B preparations can be impossible to implement. Today we'll look at how we can regard such challenges as opportunities.

Strategies

I wonder if you've missed a day since we started this program? If so, that is nothing to worry about, and it's certainly not a reason to give up. It's just an initial stumble as we find our way on the path. The more strategies we internalize and practice, the more support there is for the meditation habit, and eventually we get to the point where missing a day becomes unthinkable. But we can only accumulate the strategies that support a Rock-Solid Daily Meditation Practice gradually. At the beginning, when we're still working out how to use these skills, and working out how to remember to use them, it's easy for us to falter.

This is especially the case when we encounter major disruptions to our lives. I'm talking about things that go beyond the normal plan B interruptions to your schedule. For example, you might be on a long road trip where you're driving a lot and never alone, or your routine might be upside down because of guests staying, or a family member might be sick and you spend the whole day in the ER waiting room. These major upsets to our routine can throw us off our stride and make us forget about our commitment to sitting. Some major upset to your schedule is certain to happen at some point, and you should think about how you can stay faithful to your intention to practice.

Keep up the mantra! It reminds you of your intention to meditate every day no matter what. And with that intention in mind, keep finding a way to practice. Be creative. You can meditate in the passenger seat of the car while someone else is driving. (Obviously, talk to the driver about what you're going to do so that they won't keep interrupting you.) You can meditate in the ER. You can meditate standing up, looking out of a window. You can meditate in a bathroom stall. You can meditate in an airplane seat. Don't use the absence of "perfect conditions" as an excuse not to sit.

Don't let social awkwardness get in the way of sitting, either. I used to find that when I had visitors or was visiting people, I would want to avoid looking weird and antisocial by going off to meditate, and so I might end up missing a day. Looking back on those slip-ups, I realized that all I had to do was to say to my host (or guests), "You know, I've been working on the habit of meditating every day, and I want to keep that up, so if you don't mind, I'm going to slip off to my room for ten minutes." No one has ever been anything but supportive. (Probably they've even enjoyed an opportunity to be alone.)

You should also reflect on how to handle a setback so that you don't become overly discouraged and give up. I've found it helpful to adopt the viewpoint that when we slip up, we're not doing an easy thing badly, but instead are working out how to do something difficult. Slip-ups are inevitable. They're part of the process. Setbacks are opportunities to learn. When you slip up and miss a day, don't waste time blaming yourself. Tell yourself it's OK, but also think about how you might do things differently in the future.

In a *Scientific American* article on keeping New Year's resolutions, writer Michele Solis suggested that we see developing a new habit as an adventure, with setbacks as interesting plot twists.[28] Seeing the cultivation of a new habit as more like an adventure or a game helps us to take it less personally. The point of an adventure is to find your way through, no matter what. So make that happen.

"I meditate every day. It's just what I do. It's part of who I am. I don't need perfect conditions."

Going Deeper

The mantra that we've been using—"I meditate every day. It's just what I do. It's part of who I am"—helps us awaken and cultivate an important spiritual quality called *appamāda*. There's no universal agreement on how to translate *appamāda*, but I'm going to call it "diligence." This is one of the commoner translations, although you'll also find it rendered as "heedfulness," "non-neglectfulness," "conscientiousness," or "vigilance." Although these words have different shades of meaning, they all involve taking immediate action when we've gone astray, so that we can realign ourselves with what's good and helpful. *Appamāda* is ethical diligence. It's commitment to practice.

A very early Buddhist text, the Dhammapada, has a whole chapter on *appamāda*, the first verse of which is "Heedfulness is the state free of death; heedlessness is the state of death. The heedful do not die, while the heedless are like the dead."[29] The Buddha regarded *appamāda* as the single most important spiritual quality: "All skillful qualities are rooted in diligence, converge in diligence, and diligence is reckoned the foremost among them." Diligence, he said, is like the roof-peak that holds up the rest of a building.[30] No diligence; no practice.

Diligence has the crucial spiritual role of preventing us from straying too far into unskillful behaviors. It helps us to protect and nourish our skillful qualities. The opposite of diligence is *pamāda*, meaning heedlessness, carelessness, negligence, indolence, and even literal drunkenness. A drunk person becomes clumsy, careless, and forgetful. Their sense of priorities changes when they're intoxicated, so that they might do things they would normally consider to be wrong. To have *appamāda* is to sober up spiritually, bringing ourselves back on track.

Our mantra helps us cultivate diligence. When we tell ourselves repeatedly that meditating daily is just what we do, we create a self-view that supports daily meditation. Let's say we arrive at the end of the day and realize that we haven't yet sat. We remember, "I meditate every day. It's just what I do. It's part of who I am." Diligence has arisen, and now it seems natural to meditate. So we sit, even if it's just for a few minutes. We've stayed on track. At the end of our period of sitting practice, we're glad that we've stayed true to ourselves and to our intention to sit every day. We feel good about ourselves.

In contrast, when we carry around thoughts such as, "I've tried meditating every day. It just doesn't work for me," we're giving ourselves an out. When we're presented with the opportunity to miss a day's meditation, we've already given ourselves permission to surrender to passivity and lethargy. We end up not meditating because that conforms to our view that we don't meditate every day. We fail to act diligently.

Our mantra helps us move from a mere *intention* to sit daily, which we may or may not follow through on, to developing a *commitment* to sit daily. An intention may be nothing more than a halfhearted wish, amounting to something like "It would be nice if I meditated daily." Commitment, however, is "I meditate every day. I find a way. I don't miss days." Good intentions can feel pleasant in the short term because they allow us to feel virtuous without necessarily doing anything. We initially feel good because we're thinking about doing something good. But we end up feeling bad about ourselves because we fail to follow through. A commitment goes far beyond an intention. It's a promise we make to ourselves and that we hold ourselves to. It's dedication to a course of action. It's a determination to remain true to ourselves.

The Buddha pointed out that good intentions aren't enough. He said that if someone lacks diligence, then even if they intend to practice spiritually, they fail to make any actual progress. They can't stay committed, so that everything they do is halfhearted. Yet another person who has diligence, even if they have no stronger an intention than the first person—ends up making real progress.[31]

If we follow through on our commitment to sit daily, we feel good about ourselves, not because we think it makes us look good, but because we've truly accomplished something. We've acted with integrity. We've stayed faithful to our practice.

Having diligence doesn't mean being perfect and never making mistakes. It means recognizing and learning from our mistakes. You will at some point slip up and have a day when you forget to meditate. That might happen next year, next week, or even today. (By the way, have you sat today?) These setbacks are opportunities for us to cultivate diligence by recommitting ourselves to practice as soon as we can.

We need to actively cultivate diligence. And that means coming back to our mantra over and other again, repeating it until we believe it to be true: "I *do* meditate every day. It *is* just what I do. It *is* part of who I am." When I write about diligence, it might sound like I'm talking about willpower. It sometimes sounds like that to me. I have to remind myself that I'm not. I'm not talking about forcing ourselves to do something with the muscular might of our will. I'm talking about keeping in mind what we want to achieve and intelligently—almost cunningly—finding ways to motivate ourselves.

Our mantra creates a self-view that gets us practicing daily, not because we force ourselves to but because it's natural. By changing how we see ourselves, we bring diligence into being. And diligence, as the "path to the deathless," helps bring all other skillful qualities into being. When we cultivate diligence by repeating our mantra, all other spiritual qualities follow.

Reflection

It's easy for us to go through life on autopilot. One way you can remind yourself to come back to mindful awareness is to ask yourself the question "Am I aware of being aware?" If you consciously ask yourself this question a few times in the next hour or so, you may well find that it starts to arise spontaneously in daily life. The great thing about this is that you can't fail. As soon as the thought, "Am I aware of being aware?" comes into your mind, you are already aware of being aware. You're already mindful. You can always write those words on a Post-it note and put it somewhere you're likely to see it. Try moving it to a different place every day so that you don't tune it out.

Last Words

The Buddha's final advice to his followers before he died was "Strive diligently" (*appamādena sampādetha*). He didn't use his last words to tell them to have faith. He didn't tell them to be mindful. He left them with the exhortation to practice with diligence. That's how important it is, and that's what you're developing as you learn to meditate every day, no matter what.

DAY 13

Adopt a Growth Mindset

Practice Reminder

Remember to sit, even if it's just for five minutes. It's just what you do. Then celebrate, and record your progress.

Today

Embrace your ability to grow and change. Recognize the stories you tell yourself about your limitations, and recognize that they are just that—stories. The more you recognize this, the less hold these limiting self-views have on you.

Strategies

Stanford researcher Carol Dweck has explored how some of us develop views about our capabilities being static, so that we believe that our intelligence, abilities, and skills are inherently stable and unchangeable. We may believe we have a limited capacity for growth and change, and so we assume, for example, that if we're not good at math then we never can be. "I'm not good at math" becomes one of the stories we tell about ourselves. Dweck calls this having a "fixed mindset." Others, however, see themselves as capable of change. They believe that their intelligence, abilities, and skills are not carved in stone, but can be developed through the intelligent application of practice. Dweck calls this the "growth mindset." Having a belief in the possibility of growth allows for growth.[32]

Dweck's area of expertise is education. She's found that children with a fixed mindset believe that their intelligence level is an immutable characteristic. When they discover that there's something they can't do, they assume that they're just "not smart enough" and give up. Children with a growth mindset, on the other hand, see intellectual ability as a set of learned skills or strategies. When they find there's something they can't do, they look for a new strategy. The two groups relate differently to feelings of frustration. Kids with a fixed mindset see frustration as a sign of being unable to learn. They take it as a signal that they should stop trying. Those with a growth mindset see frustration as a sign that they are learning. Much as a weightlifter would see pain as a sign of building muscles as they pump iron, people with a growth mindset see frustration as a sign of learning. Not surprisingly, students with a growth mindset tend to do much better in school.

Dweck has found that children with a fixed mindset can learn to adopt a growth mindset if they are taught that the brain is capable of change. She found that a brief intervention in which kids learn that the brain is "plastic"—that it is not fixed, but instead rewires itself and even grows as we learn—boosts their academic performance more than giving them a study skills class. Having embraced the reality that their intellectual capacity is capable of growth, they become more confident and curious, and are more inspired to keep trying new strategies and practice skills until they finally understand things that had eluded them.

If we have the idea that an inability to sustain a daily meditation practice is a fixed part of who we are, then we don't change. We take setbacks as a confirmation of our fixed mindset belief: "If it's hard, that means I can't do it." If we adopt a growth mindset, on the other hand, then we'll take setbacks as a sign that we need to learn new strategies, or to look again at those we already know to see how we can apply them: "If it's hard, that means I need to keep trying."

We can speed up the adoption of a growth mindset if we reflect on the nature of the brain in the same way that Dweck encouraged fixed-mindset children to do. Scientists used to believe that after an initial phase of growth in early life, the brain settled down into being a static network of neurons, not that different from the fixed wiring in a computer. And then they discovered that London cabbies, who had to navigate the vast maze of their city, had much larger "navigation modules" in their brains than the average person. Maybe people who already happened to have brains that were good at navigation were more likely to become taxi drivers? Well, the longer people had been in the job, the larger the navigational parts of their brains became. It seems that the brain does indeed change and grow in response to learning. This doesn't just apply to learning to navigate; the practice of meditation promotes growth in the parts of the brain associated with self-control, compassion, and happiness.

Every time we sit down to meditate, let's visualize our brains changing, imagining that the neural pathways of the meditation habit strengthen, sit by sit. Rewiring the brain happens a little at a time, but it happens. Every sit makes a difference. We've seen that the Buddha observed that gradual changes we might dismiss as insignificant can nevertheless produce life-changing results. One drop at a time, a water jug becomes full.

Embracing a growth mindset, which we've been doing throughout this book, is itself a powerful strategy for getting our sit together and developing a Rock-Solid Daily Meditation Practice. The Buddhist tradition says that there is no such thing as a fixed self, and that everything that constitutes who we are is in a process of change. There is fundamentally nothing about us that is absolutely fixed. One of the biggest favors we can do for ourselves is to embrace this reality.

"I meditate every day. It's just what I do. It's part of who I am. I embrace my ability to change."

Going Deeper

Early Buddhist texts talk about enlightenment as a process, unfolding in stages. The first stage of enlightenment is called "stream entry" and involves breaking three fetters. The first of those fetters is "self-view." (The other two are "doubt," and "clinging to ethical rules and religious practices as ends in themselves," each of which we'll look at later.) These fetters all break at the same time, and the moment they do is the beginning of a new phase of our lives. When this happens, we've reached a tipping point. We've had an insight into how things really are, and this insight can never be lost. We are now on the path of no return. We're on the way to full enlightenment.

This change essentially involves a move from a spiritual fixed mindset, where we believe that we have a permanent and unchanging self, to a spiritual growth mindset, where we realize that every aspect of our being is changing all the time, and that we have all the conditions necessary for continued growth until enlightenment. All of this is to do with how we see the "self."

In Pali, "self-view" is *sakkāya-diṭṭhi*, which literally means "the view (*diṭṭhi*) that there is a real (*sat*) body (*kāya*)." The "body" that's referred to here isn't the physical body we can see and touch and put deodorant on, but an imagined entity, which we call a self. We see this imagined self as having a number of characteristics, all of which are contrary to fact.

> *The self is our essence.* It's some part of us that doesn't change and so is able to provide continuity from day to day and year to year. As the essence of who we are, it's the bearer of the qualities that make us up and define us.

> *The self is unified.* The self that perceives situations is the same self that responds to them. The self that suffers is the same self that offers itself compassion. We're aware of a certain lack of unity

within ourselves ("I really need to get out of bed! *Just five more minutes!*") but we usually dismiss it, usually by seeing one of our inner voices as the "real us" and the other one as a disruptive intruder.

The self is what acts. It's what feels, remembers, thinks, decides, and makes things happen in our lives. We assume if we didn't have such a self, we wouldn't be able to do anything.

The self exists separately. It exists independently of the world around it. We usually think our own self is more important than almost anything or anyone else.

This is not how the self is, because nothing like that exists. This is just how we imagine ourselves to be.

The way we imagine the self is not that different to how people in the past imagined nature to have a self, or selves, in the form of nature spirits, deities, and God himself. "How could the sun rise and set, the tides ebb and flow, and the seasons roll on from year to year if there were no gods?" they thought. (Of course some still do.) Similarly, we mistakenly think of the self as like a little god within us—an inner deity that makes everything happen. It's the *real* body within the body (the *sat-kāya*). It's a "mini-me"—a supposed being dwelling within us, defining who we are, thinking, feeling, and acting.

This self we imagine to be within us simply doesn't exist. Returning to the four characteristics of the supposed self that I outlined above:

An unchanging self can't exist. Neuroscientists say that the brain is constantly remodeling itself, and there's no place within it that an unchanging entity could exist.

A unified self can't exist. The brain doesn't have the kind of unified structure that would allow for a "mini-me," deity-like self that's in charge of everything.

There is no one "agent" within our being. Various parts of the brain exist and function independently of each other. Notice, for example, how surprised you are when your body catches a falling object without you "asking" it to.

The self cannot be independent. Our bodies and minds do not exist separately from the world. They are formed from the world and can never be separated from it. We are in a state of total, ongoing, constantly shifting relatedness.

The belief in a fixed self is a significant spiritual problem. As long as we assume that our inner essence is something unchanging, we doubt our ability to change. We do observe ourselves changing—becoming kinder, perhaps—but fundamentally we doubt that we can become awakened. This doubt is the second of the fetters that holds us back.

Since the kind of self we think we have doesn't exist, we don't need to get rid of it, any more than we need to get rid of the monsters under the bed we were terrified of as children. You can't get rid of something that doesn't exist; you can only stop believing in it. An important part of spiritual practice is learning to see that what doesn't exist in fact doesn't exist.

This isn't easy to do, because our belief that we have a self of the kind I've described is deep-rooted and stubborn. But if, making a good-faith effort, we keep accumulating evidence that contradicts a belief, we eventually have to abandon the belief. We eventually stop believing in the self. We can become atheistic with regard to our inner gods.

First, keep *directly looking at and reflecting on your experience.* Are you really the same person you were when you were a fetus or a baby, or when you were ten years old? Where, then is the unchanging essence?

Reflect on the fact that every atom in your body has come from the outside world.

Notice how it makes no sense to consider yourself as absolutely separate from the world. Can you be happy if your relationships with others are in a state of conflict? Have you ever heard anyone say, "I love my job, but I can't stand my boss or any of the people I work with"? Notice the ways in which your practice is a collaborative effort—how you have to learn from others, not just in terms of intellectual knowledge that's passed on, but also by way of learning by example. We see someone being kinder or more patient than we would normally be, and it inspires us to believe we could do similar things.

Above all, observe how everything in your experience, including your consciousness, is in a constant state of change. No sensation is the same from one moment to the next. Thoughts come and go constantly. Your feelings consist of an ever-changing pattern of inner sensation as nerve endings wink on and off with incredible rapidity within the body. Notice all this, and keep asking yourself, "Where, in all this change, could an unchanging self reside?"

When you stop believing in the existence of this self that doesn't exist—and this will happen someday if you keep practicing sincerely—*you* don't stop existing. You, in all your undefinable complexity and mystery, are still there, but you contain one less illusion. And the loss of that delusion is a good loss, because your belief in a self did not make you happy. Because suffering kept arising, the self you imagined you had seemed to be fundamentally flawed. And that brought up the question, how could anyone possibly drag the weight of such a broken self all the way along the path to enlightenment? Surely you are unworthy and incapable of perfection?

The good news is you only thought you were dragging this weight around. It never really existed. You're like a mime who's acted out being trapped in a box so long that you really believe you're trapped. I'm happy to tell you that the box is imaginary.

The belief that says "I can't meditate every day. I'm just not cut out for it. I don't have what it takes" is the fetter of doubt. In turn that's an expression of the fetter of self-view. It's a fixed mindset.

In contrast, "I meditate every day. It's just what I do. It's part of who I am" helps us to break that fetter. It commits us to the path of practice. And our practice, if we stick with it, will eventually help us to see through our delusions. Practice frees us, despite ourselves.

Reflection

One of my favorite ways of undermining the notion that there is a self that's responsible for everything I do is to catch my body doing things without it being explicitly asked to. Right now, for example, I'm noticing how, when words appear in my mind, my fingers fly to the appropriate letters on my keyboard. I don't make my fingers move. I don't even know how the words arise. Similarly, I notice how my body drives a car, walks, and breathes while my mind is busy with other things. Every time I notice these things, I realize that "I" (my conscious mind) is not doing any of these things. Action is happening, and yet I am not acting. Try noticing these things in your own life.

Last Words

In your meditation practice and in daily life, keep observing that all experience is experience of change. Your bodily sensations, your feelings, your thoughts are never the same from one moment to another. If you think there is some part of your experience that is unchanging, look more closely. And as you observe only change, keep asking yourself, "Where, among all this instability and impermanence, could an unchanging self exist?"

DAY 14

Support Your Practice with Ritual

Practice Reminder

Have you sat yet today? If not, why not take five minutes to do so now. Remember to celebrate: "Yay, me!" And then extend the chain on your planner.

Today

Practicing rituals before and after meditation can be deeply enriching.

Strategies

We can help ourselves establish a new habit by bringing elements of ritual—defined as spiritually significant actions performed with a sense of ceremony and dignity—into our practice.

It's good to have a special place to meditate and to mark the specialness of that place by decorating it with spiritually meaningful items. This doesn't have to be elaborate. I meditate in my office, and I have a small Buddha statue, some flowers, candles, and a bowl for burning incense. I get pleasure from lighting the candles and placing a stick of lighted incense upright in the bowl. These things can be done with a mindful awareness of my bodily movements, my feelings, and my senses, so that my meditation practice begins even before I sit down.

Bowing, usually before and after lighting the candles and incense, invokes a spirit of receptivity toward the teachings. It's also a sign of gratitude toward the Buddha and other enlightened teachers. The Buddha statue is esthetically pleasing, and is also a reminder of the goal of becoming a wiser and more compassionate human being. If you're not a Buddhist, you can find some other reminder of your ideals. Flowers, candles, and incense have symbolic resonances as well. Flowers represent the opening of the human heart, and the Buddha's awakened state. Candles represent the way the Buddha's teachings illuminate the world with wisdom. Incense smoke, as it drifts into the world, symbolizes how the effects of our practice permeate the world.

The flickering light of candles is pleasing, as is the scent of the incense, which enlivens my senses and helps me be more aware of my breathing. The scent of the incense evokes states of calm and joy I have experienced in past meditations.

Some people like to chant at the beginning of a meditation. This too can be a kind of premeditation meditation. Buddhists often chant the refuges and precepts, for example, which establish the context and purpose of our practice—that is, to wake up to reality and to live in a way that benefits both ourselves and others. I include a version of these in appendix 1. At the end of the sit there is a sense of ceremony as I extinguish the candles. You might want to give another bow then, or to say a few words of prayerful intention. Most Buddhist traditions have some form of "dedicating merit." So you could say something simple like "May all beings, without limit, benefit from this practice," or chant something more elaborate, like the "Dedication of Merit" verses you'll also find in appendix 1. These words remind us that we're not meditating simply to become happier ourselves, but so that we can help others be happier too.

Every time you see your meditation altar, or even just your cushions or bench, can be a reminder of your intention to practice daily. The smell of incense can do the same thing. It's the first thing I notice when I walk into my home, and every time I smell it on my clothing it reminds me of my meditation practice and of the peace that arises from it.

Ritual can be an entire practice in itself—in Tibetan temples, devotional rituals can go on for hours—but it can also frame and support your daily meditation practice, bringing to mind the wider spiritual context in which it exists.

"I meditate every day. It's just what I do. It's part of who I am. I sit for the benefit of all beings."

Going Deeper

A few weeks after I'd first begun attending classes at the Glasgow Buddhist Center in my native Scotland, I'd developed enough of a connection with the people there that I was invited to attend a regulars' evening. While the format of the introductory classes had been purposely secular—designed to appeal to the widest possible range of people—the regulars' gathering was more overtly religious. Before the meditation there was bowing and chanting. After the main event, which was a talk, there was a collective *puja*, or act of worship, in which we recited verses together and chanted mantras. Some people offered lighted sticks of incense to the Buddha. I had no idea what any of this meant, and although I was intrigued, I was also rather uncomfortable. I remember wondering if all this was necessary. Wasn't meditating enough? Wasn't all this a bit superstitious and cult-like?

I came to enjoy ritual practices, but many people, when they first come across it, share my initial misgivings. Many of us who are brought up in a secular culture are attracted to Buddhism because of its reputation as a rational religious tradition. We can be uncomfortable with ritual. We may see bowing as an act of subservience. Eventually I came to understand that ritual is not meaningless and isn't about obedience to authority. It isn't a cult activity. Instead, ritual is a spiritual practice like any other.

Chanting is a mindfulness practice. While chanting, we can be aware of the body, the breathing, and the movements that take place in the mouth and throat as we create sound. We can be mindful of the meaning of the words we're saying. We can be mindful of how we feel as we say them. If we're chanting with others then we can be mindful of them too, so that we harmonize and synchronize with each other.

Bowing is a practice of respect. It's not about obedience or about saying that we're inferior. If you and I were both Japanese and we met on the street, we'd naturally bow to each other. It's a gesture that embodies the mutual recognition that we are living beings that *matter*. A lot of Dharma practitioners in the West bow to each other, in fact, although mostly in Buddhist contexts rather than on the high street. We find it a gracious way to acknowledge each other. It's similar when we bow to some representation of enlightenment, such as a Buddha statue. The statue is a reminder of the Buddha as a historical individual. If we were to meet him, we'd naturally want to show him respect. Bowing to a Buddha statue doesn't mean we are demeaning ourselves. We are simply acknowledging that the Buddha had deep insights and qualities of character that we respect and want to emulate. And that's what the statue is; it's a reminder that enlightenment is possible, and that it's possible because of all the hard work the Buddha did on our behalf. Bowing expresses our gratitude for all that.

I've heard many people say that the first time they bowed to a representation of the Buddha, they felt that a bubble of egotism "popped." They've realized that their resistance to physical demonstrations of gratitude toward the Buddha had been a form of clinging to self. We've talked about the delusion of the self. We imagine that we have one, and we assume that other people have one too. And we naturally start comparing selves, ranking our own imagined self as being better or worse than others' selves. The Buddha called this "conceit." Now in English, having conceit means you think you're superior to others, but for the Buddha, conceit also covers believing that you are inferior to others. In both cases you're using comparison to reinforce your conception of having a self.

We might think that if we're to eschew assumptions of inferiority and superiority, we need to think of ourselves as being equal to everyone else, but the Buddha regarded even that comparison as being a form of conceit. Believing we have a self that can be evaluated against other selves *in any way whatsoever* is still reinforcing the notion that we have a self, strengthening the fetter of self-view, creating more suffering for ourselves, and making it even harder to become enlightened. In bowing to the Buddha, we're letting go of any ideas of our own superiority or inferiority, and simply saying "thank you" for the gift of the Dharma.

Even the Buddha felt reverence. Just after he became enlightened, as he sat in seclusion, still absorbing the impact of what had happened to him, he had the thought, "It's unpleasant to live without respect and reverence."[33] No one in the world surpassed him in spiritual development, but there was still some *thing* for him to revere: "Why don't I honor and respect and rely on the same Dhamma to which I was awakened?" he thought.

The Buddha saw reverence and respect as a necessary part of a healthy human life. Reverence opens a kind of spiritual portal that allows movement in two directions. On the one hand, our respect flows, as gratitude, toward whoever or whatever it is that we respect. But we also become more open to being influenced by them—more receptive to the influence of whoever or whatever it is that we respect.

The Buddha was talking about this two-way flow when he said, "Respect and humility, contentment and gratitude, and timely listening to the teaching: this is the highest blessing."[34] Respect is the way we relate to those who have benefited us. Humility is letting go of our egotistic ideas of equality. Contentment is the sense of ease that arises from doing this. Gratitude is what we feel as we acknowledge how we benefit. And because of our openness, we become wholeheartedly receptive to the teachings.

Reflection

Who have you respected and had reverence for over the course of your life? These may be people who are famous, or people you've known personally. They might even be fictional characters, like Gandalf from *The Lord of the Rings*, or Wonder Woman. Whose photographs, for example, have you chosen to have on display? Whose quotes have you cherished? Who have you wished you could be more like? Reflect on or write about the qualities that made these people your heroes.

Last Words

In our secular age, it can be hard to begin practicing reverence. But we can start small, with an image of the Buddha or some other spiritual figure. Then we can light candles and incense in a mindful way. We might read a poem or a few lines of scripture, and eventually graduate to making a bow of gratitude before and after sitting.

DAY 15

Outsmart Your Resistance

Practice Reminder

If you haven't sat yet today, then this may be a good time for it. Remember that meditating is more important than reading about meditating. So sit, celebrate, and record your progress!

Today

Feeling resistant to meditating is something that happens to us all at some point. As you read today's chapter, remember times that you've avoided sitting, and mentally rehearse how you could relate more mindfully to such resistance the next time it manifests in your life.

Strategies

We've all experienced resistance toward meditation—that sinking feeling when sitting is the last thing you want to do, and when you'd rather surf the internet, have a cup of coffee, or even clean the bathroom rather than get your butt on the cushion. Arguing with this resistance is rarely productive. When you confront the thought, "I can't be bothered to meditate" with the thought, "I really should meditate," then you're in an argument. And your resistance will almost always win that kind of fight. Your resistance has had a whole lifetime of training in outsmarting you, and it is captain of your inner debate team. We need other approaches.

To begin with, stop focusing on the stories your mind is telling you, like "Ugh, I don't want to meditate. I'll do it tomorrow." Instead, focus on what's going on in the body. When we have resistance, there are always unpleasant feelings present. Notice them and be curious about them. What feelings are they? Anxiety? Restlessness? Dread? As best you can, accept them and investigate them—not by thinking about them, but by observing them closely as sensations. Where are they located? Perhaps in the pit of the stomach? Around the heart? Maybe a generalized feeling of heaviness throughout the body? What texture do they have? Are their boundaries clear or fuzzy? Are they stable or changing?

Don't try to banish or fix your resistance. Just observe its feelings as if they were any other sensations, such as the sensations of your breathing or the weight of your body pressing into the earth. Approach your feelings without judgment. Approach them with kindness, empathy, curiosity, and a desire simply to be with them. Let them be old friends you're sitting with companionably. Notice the breathing as well, as it sweeps in soft waves of movement and sensation through the body. You're just breathing, and noticing the sensations of resistance. Observe all this with a little kindness. Your resistance is not your enemy. It's just a part of you that's fearful.

The interesting thing is that if you're being mindful of your resistance, you're already meditating. Even if you're exploring this resistance while you're standing in the kitchen, poised to pour yourself a distracting cup of coffee, you're meditating. At that point you can simply set down the coffee pot, close your eyes, and do five minutes of standing meditation. If you're sitting at the computer or slumped on the couch with your phone, and you're investigating the felt qualities of your resistance, you're meditating. You're practicing right there, right then. So just keep going. If you feel moved to get up and go to your meditation space, feel free. Otherwise just keep practicing where you are. Your resistance may pass, and you can continue with your practice as you normally do. Or perhaps it won't, and you just stay present with it: breathing in, noticing the resistance; breathing out, noticing the resistance.

Resistance need not be an obstacle to your meditation practice. It can instead be the object of your meditation practice, part of your meditation practice. It's just one more experience that you can mindfully and compassionately observe. So instead of arguing with your resistance, outsmart it by surrounding it with mindful awareness. Your resistance may be able to run rings around you in an argument, but it has no idea know how to deal with being observed mindfully.

Outsmarting our resistance is empowering. It helps us feel confident, strong, and happy. Resistance is perhaps our biggest obstacle to meditating daily, and if we can overcome that, there is no holding us back. The curiosity that helps us to overcome resistance is another thing that feels pleasant. The pleasure of curiosity and of victory over resistance become part of our reward system, reminding us that meditating is a good thing to do, something we want to do, and something we're drawn to. This feeds into the reward system that keeps us practicing.

"I meditate every day. It's just what I do. It's part of who I am. I see resistance as an ally on the path."

Going Deeper

I remember reading a famous case about a man who had sustained an unusual form of brain damage that stopped him from being able to access his feelings. You might imagine that someone who's freed from emotion would be a coolly effective and logical being, like Mr. Spock from *Star Trek*. But in fact this man had great difficulty functioning in daily life. When his therapist would try to arrange their next meeting, for example, the patient would look at all the available dates, trying to work out which one would *logically* be the best. And he couldn't do this because the task was simply too complicated. How to choose? There were too many variables.

The human brain has not evolved to work like a computer running database calculations, consciously comparing multiple options in a quantitative way. Instead, when we need to make a complex decision involving multiple variables, the brain takes a kinesthetic shortcut. Our "computing" takes place out of sight and out of mind, and the results of its calculations are presented to us in terms of feelings. You think of one option ("Maybe Monday would work?") and there might be something like a slight sinking feeling in the heart. Think of another ("How about Tuesday?") and there might be a pleasant sense of softness, energy, and warmth instead, or just a neutral feeling that lets you know there's no problem with that date.

Our gut responses have a profound role in shaping our decisions. Psychologists have shown that within a tenth of a second of seeing someone, or even just of seeing a photograph of them, we have formed opinions about things like their likeability, trustworthiness, and competence. In most cases we're not aware we've made these instantaneous assessments, but we're aware of the feelings that arise in the body. We might feel a warm glow of approval for one person, or tightness and distaste for another. We can't get through life without these heuristic shortcuts. Our unconscious mind is like a GPS that steers our decisions, not by showing us on a map or giving verbal commands, but by using the language of inner sensation.

We often barely notice our feelings, probably because we're more concerned about the real-world decisions we are making than in the underlying sensations that guide them. You feel like Chinese rather than Thai; who cares about the sensations guiding that choice? So we take our feelings for granted, which means we're often making decisions based not on thoughtful analysis but on hunches. That may be fine for deciding what's for dinner, but we often have aversion toward actions that affect our well-being. The resistance that we discussed yesterday is one example. Going through life on autopilot, we allow our unconscious minds to manipulate us into making decisions that may in many instances be unwise.

When we're mindful of our feelings, we gain more freedom to question whether they're pushing us in helpful directions. We can consider what promotes our own and others' long-term happiness and well-being. We can recognize that although our feelings may be trying to manipulate us to avoid meditation, we don't have to go along with that course of action. When we feel resistance, the information our unconscious mind is offering us about meditation isn't based on what's best for us. In fact, it often seems to be that our resistance comes from parts of the mind that dread the prospect of positive change. When we're mindful of our feelings, we are uncoupling them from our decision making. We no longer react automatically, but instead respond more consciously and wisely. This is why being mindful of our feelings is such a powerful practice.

Reflection

As you go through your day, practice being more aware of the feelings that inform—and often compel—your actions. These will usually be found in the chest and abdomen. Observing feelings as they come and go in our daily lives can be fascinating and liberating.

Last Words

Whether you're deciding what day to meet your therapist, choosing a dish at a restaurant, or trying to work out if you should trust a stranger, you rely largely on your feelings. Bringing more mindfulness to your feelings helps your decision making to be more conscious, rational, and probably more beneficial in the long term.

DAY 16

Be Kind to Future You

Practice Reminder

You meditate every day. It's just what you do. It's part of who you are. So check to make sure it's happening today if it hasn't already. Then celebrate to generate pleasant feelings about sitting. And joyfully record today's sit in your meditation planner.

Today

We create problems for ourselves with unhelpful habits. For example, we might have a habit of staying up late, so we're either sleep-deprived in the morning or we sleep in and don't have time to practice. Using willpower to change those habits is rarely successful, so let's look at how we can change them using self-compassion.

Strategies

Sometimes I used to be about to go to bed, and to my dismay I'd notice that there were still a few dishes lying in the sink from the kids' bedtime snacks. Evening Bodhi would think, "Ugh. I'll leave them for Morning Bodhi to do!" The next day, Morning Bodhi wasn't happy that Evening Bodhi had left him (Morning Bodhi) with a crusty pile of dishes to deal with.

Not only that, but Evening Bodhi had stayed up late, and now Morning Bodhi was stuck not only with the dishes, but also with the exhaustion of being sleep-deprived. Morning Bodhi thought Evening

Bodhi hadn't been kind or thoughtful. Unfortunately, Evening Bodhi hadn't thought much about Morning Bodhi at all. In fact, he tended to take him for granted. The two didn't have a very friendly relationship with one another.

This was all highly unsatisfactory, and since I liked both of those guys and wanted them to get on with each other, I started encouraging Evening Bodhi to develop more empathy for Morning Bodhi. This started having an effect. Last night, for example, Evening Bodhi was watching an engrossing sci-fi show and was contemplating watching just one more episode, when he thought, "You know, that's going to keep me up late, and that's going to make Morning Bodhi feel horrible." Then Evening Bodhi noticed some dirty dishes, and decided to be kind to Morning Bodhi, not just by going to bed on time but by cleaning up for him as well.

Evening Bodhi had always assumed that the less housework he did, the happier he'd be, but to his surprise he even enjoyed clearing away those dishes. Knowing he was doing a favor for someone else turned what was normally an unpleasant chore into a pleasurable activity. It turns out that Evening Bodhi enjoyed doing nice things for Morning Bodhi. And Morning Bodhi was delighted that Evening Bodhi had started being more thoughtful and considerate.

The thing about getting to bed early is that it's a big challenge for Evening Bodhi. He's good at chilling, but isn't always good at knowing when to stop. And when he stays up too late, Morning Bodhi doesn't have much time for meditation, and he doesn't enjoy struggling to stay awake. When Evening Bodhi realized that Morning Bodhi was a real person with needs and feelings, he naturally wanted to get to bed at a reasonable hour. Evening Bodhi and Morning Bodhi are more like friends now, while in the past they used to be more like uncooperative roommates who'd exchange passive-aggressive messages. (For some strange reason they never seem to bump into each other.) So now

Morning Bodhi has more time to meditate, and he's not so tired, so his meditation practice is much more pleasant.

On those few days when Bodhi isn't able to meditate until the evening (one of those plan B things), he's sometimes tempted to just do just a five-minute sit, but sometimes he thinks about how proud Morning Bodhi will be of him if he does twenty minutes instead. And yes, the next day, Morning Bodhi looks back at the practice his strangely absent roommate has done and thinks, "Good for you, dude!" and feels happy about it.

Somehow, Evening Bodhi's practice seems to influence Morning Bodhi's moods. And Morning Bodhi being able to meditate more somehow affects Evening Bodhi, making it easier for him to exert more control over his TV habits. (Maybe it's some kind of spooky psychic thing.)

What I'm describing is self-empathy, which means treating yourself as a feeling being who experiences happiness and unhappiness and who is worthy of respect and kindness. Not only is your well-being and happiness important right now, but the well-being and happiness of your future self is important too. Your future self feels joy and pain just as you do, and is worthy of being treated well. Let yourself feel kindness toward them. Cultivating a relationship of respect and gratitude between your present, future, and past selves will bring much more harmony and joy into your life. So just think of your future self as a real person with real feelings and treat them considerately. Think about how your actions might affect them.

Disruptive habits are more easily changed with kindness than with self-criticism. So if you're ever tempted to skip meditation, think how Future You will feel about it. They're probably going to be much happier if you get your butt on the cushion, stay faithful to your practice, and don't break the chain. Future You will look back with gratitude at the helpful things Past You has done for them. Those two could really start to like each other and work well together. In fact, I have a feeling this may be the beginning of a beautiful friendship!

"I meditate every day. It's just what I do. It's part of who I am. And I practice with kindness toward my future self."

Going Deeper

Of all the practices I've learned, self-compassion has transformed my life more than any other—more, even, than mindfulness. I've shared how we can bring more respect and kindness into the way our evening selves and our morning selves relate to each other, but I'd also like to outline a simple but powerful five-step practice of self-compassion that you can bring into any moment of suffering.

1. Recognize That You're Suffering

When we're suffering, you'd think it would be obvious that we're suffering, but often it isn't. When we think about what it is to suffer, we often think of major difficulties, such as being in a war zone, having cancer, or grieving the loss of a loved one. But suffering is something we experience all the time. We worry about what people think about us. We get hurt when we're ignored. We feel bored standing in line. We get frustrated at poor customer service or a slow internet connection. We get angry at people who drive badly. These are all forms of suffering.

You might think, "Yeah, but those things are so minor! They're not real suffering!" And, sure, there are much more painful things in life. But these are the forms of suffering we have most often. There's often just one thing after another. Sometimes it seems our whole life is spent wading through minor sufferings, and these little dings against our sense of well-being can leave us feeling worn down and miserable.

So, first we have to train ourselves to recognize: *This is a moment of suffering.*

2. Drop the Story

There's also the fact that mentally we often can't let go. We take one small incident of hurt feelings and run it in our minds like a tape loop over and over. Every time we do so we not only experience the initial hurt again, but also add new suffering. If someone cuts us off in traffic, we might imagine getting revenge, or alarm ourselves by imagining what would have happened if they'd collided with us. The secondary suffering caused by such ruminations can accumulate until we find ourselves in states of profound despair, anxiety, or chronic anger.

The Buddha said that the initial suffering we experience (whether that's stubbing our toe or being snubbed) is like being shot like an arrow. The stories we tell ourselves—"This is terrible! My life sucks!"—multiply those sufferings. He said this was like being shot by another arrow. Actually, he was understating things, because we seem to *love* using those second arrows, stabbing ourselves with them repeatedly.

So we recognize that we're making things worse for ourselves by telling these stories, and we drop them.

3. Drop Down Into the Body

We turn our attention from the proliferating stories we're creating in our minds, and pay attention instead to the painful feelings that have arisen in our bodies. When we're suffering, there is inevitably a feeling of discomfort somewhere—usually around the heart, the diaphragm, or in the gut. There are familiar descriptions for some of these feelings, as when we talk about our heart sinking, butterflies in the tummy, having the wind knocked out of us, feeling hurt, and so on. This is our primary suffering. This is the first arrow. This is what our proliferating thoughts of revenge and self-pity are reacting against.

4. Accept Your Feelings

In being mindful of feelings, as best we can we treat them as bodily sensations like any other. It's important to realize that feelings are not good or bad, but are just pleasant or unpleasant. They need to be observed, not judged. But it can be hard to persuade ourselves to move toward something painful, and when this happens we can offer ourselves reassurance, saying things like, "It's OK to feel this. This is just how I feel right now. Let me feel this. Let me simply be with this sensation." We soothe ourselves as we notice what has to be faced.

We can observe the details of these inner sensations we call feelings. What shape do they occupy in the body? Are they moving in some way? Do they seem to be exerting pressure? What surface texture do they have? Do they have weight? Do they seem solid or translucent? The more we're able to notice the details of feelings, the less we react to them and the more accepting we are.

5. Offer Support

Feelings are communications from ancient and nonverbal parts of the brain. When we're under threat, these emotional centers talk to us in the language of bodily sensation, inducing painful or at least uncomfortable sensations, usually along the midline of the body, around the heart, diaphragm, and gut. (In circumstances where a potential benefit has been detected, the sensations are instead pleasant: think of the warm glow of admiration, the pleasant ache of love, or the thrill of excitement.) This process seems to be mediated by a nerve called the vagus, which runs through those areas.

We can talk to the painful feelings that we've identified in the body. We can repeat the phrases that we might use in loving-kindness meditation, saying things like: "May you be well. May you be at ease. May you be free from suffering." Or we can have a more informal conversation, saying things like, "I know this is hard for you, but I want you to know I'm here for you. I care about you, and I want you to know we're in this together. I want you to be happy and at ease." You can if you want use these words like a kind of script, but you can also take them as suggestions for how an authentic and compassionate inner conversation might sound.

As well as talking kindly to our pain, we can enfold it in a kind field of attention. We can regard it with the inner-gaze equivalent of the way we would look at a cute animal or a newborn child. We can use touch too, placing a hand comfortingly on the part of the body where the suffering is most prominent, offering it reassurance. In meeting our pain with compassion we have many resources to draw on.

You'll find that as you offer yourself reassurance, your emotions will settle. You'll feel calmer and clearer. You discover that you can let go of your pain without obsessing about it and without firing those second arrows of secondary suffering. Other things happen too: Commonly, as we offer empathy and compassion to ourselves, those qualities become more available for others too.

This five-step practice of self-compassion can help us avoid being dragged into states of suffering, such as anxiety, anger, and despair, that can derail our good intentions and prevent us from meditating. We can also bring them into our meditation practice itself, so that we can meet painful thoughts and memories with compassion. I suggest learning these steps and practicing them so that you learn to be more self-supportive amid life's emotional challenges.

"I meditate every day. It's just what I do. It's part of who I am. I offer myself the support I need to stay true to my best intentions."

Reflection

Make a resolution to have a day in which you meet at least three moments of suffering with compassion as best you can. Record those experiences, noting what the situation was, what feelings you experienced, how you brought compassion to bear on them, how you felt afterward, and anything else that seems significant.

Last Words

Keep (1) noticing moments of suffering, (2) dropping the story, (3) dropping down into the body to observe feelings of discomfort, (4) accepting your pain, and (5) offering it support. Most times you'll find you can move on calmly and joyfully. Sometimes, especially with grief, depression, or profound anxiety, you may find that it's necessary to provide ongoing support until circumstances change.

DAY 17

Don't Wait Until You Feel Like Sitting

Practice Reminder

Sit. Celebrate. Take pleasure in adding another X to your meditation tracker.

Today

To become Rock-Solid Daily Meditators we need to overcome our habit of using transitory feelings to guide our actions. Because meditating promotes our long-term happiness and well-being, it's valuable to sit regardless of whether or not we feel like it.

Strategies

Imagine you're a monarch. You need to make decisions about how your realm will be governed, but since you can't be everywhere and know everything, you're dependent on your advisors. These advisors suggest you should take this course of action but not another. They say you should trust this person but not that one. As you listen to their counsel, you're aware that your advisors are fallible. Sometimes their perspectives are limited. Sometimes they disagree with each other. Sometimes they're biased. Sometimes they scheme and plot, trying to manipulate you for their own ends.

This is much the situation we find ourselves in while dealing with feelings. They give us information. In fact the Pali word for feeling, *vedana*, is from a verb meaning "to know." Sometimes that information is reliable and sometimes it isn't. Sometimes our feelings come from parts of the mind that are trying to manipulate us in order to further their own agendas. There are, for example, parts of the mind that don't want to change. Sometimes their advice comes from a limited perspective based on what's pleasant or unpleasant in the short term, and not on what's beneficial for you in the long term.

If you don't meditate until you feel like meditating, then you'll never establish a Rock-Solid Daily Meditation Practice. There's always going to be a time you don't feel like meditating. So don't let your feelings be the boss of you. You are the boss, the monarch. Your advisors should only advise you. Don't let them be the boss of you. Be kind to them, though. Even when their advice is terrible, you can smile, and thank them, and then go ahead and do the opposite of what they've suggested.

Some people see "don't do something unless you feel like it" as a kind of virtue. It becomes a rule of living. The idea is that if you do something you feel resistance to then you're being "inauthentic." But the question is, which part of you do you want to be authentic to? Are you being authentic to the part that is wisest and wants to develop happiness through mindfully creating inner harmony? Or are you being authentic to the part that thinks only of short-term pleasures, of taking the easy way out, and of avoiding difficult experiences?

Our lives go best when we stay true to our wisest instincts, and when we avoid being governed by impulses that don't contribute to our long-term well-being. The Buddha often considered whether a particular course of action was "for his long-term happiness and well-being." That's a phrase that comes up many times in his description of his thought processes, and when the Buddha tells you how his mind works, we really should sit up and take notice. We should probably try the same perspectives he used and see how it works out.

So, when you don't feel like meditating, meditate anyway. Find a way to motivate yourself by employing some of the strategies and tools we've learned so far:

- Do just a short sit rather than none.
- Imagine how good you'll feel after meditating.
- Meditate because you don't want to break the chain.
- Observe your resistance and meditate with it.
- Meditate because it's just what you do.
- Meditate because it's part of who you are.
- Meditate because you meditate every day.
- Meditate because "you don't miss days."
- Meditate to inspire and encourage others.
- Meditate because Tomorrow You will thank Today You.
- Meditate because it's in the interests of your long-term happiness and well-being.

Maybe you've even discovered other motivational strategies. You have plenty of ways to motivate yourself. Make a point of remembering them, and call upon them when you need them. Meditation: Just do it.

"I meditate every day. It's just what I do. It's part of who I am. I don't wait until I feel like doing it."

Going Deeper

The Buddha taught about the eight "worldly principles" or *loka-dhammas*. The later tradition called these the "worldly winds," which is a term some of you might be more familiar with. (On the principle that it's a good idea to think like the Buddha, I sometimes prefer to stick with the terminology he used—with the caveat that we're using translations.) The word *dhamma* here is the same as the word for the Buddha's teachings, but it has a different meaning. The *Buddha-dhamma* is a set of principles based on wisdom that help free us from ignorance and suffering. The *loka-dhammas* are the opposite. They are eight principles, based on misunderstanding, that bind us to suffering.

The eight principles are in four pairs:

1. Gain and loss
2. Fame and disgrace
3. Blame and praise[35]
4. Pleasure and pain

In each pair there is something we fear and try to avoid, and something we long for and try to achieve. We can see these forces at work in the world around us and within our own minds. In fact, they motivate much of our lives.

When we embrace the eight worldly principles we falsely assume that lasting happiness can be found by pursuing one item in each pair and avoiding the other. In reality, the very act of trying to find happiness within these polarities is a cause of suffering. It's through recognizing that these worldly principles can't bring happiness that we become truly happy.

The Buddha's advice was that when we encounter any of these principles in our lives, we reflect, "I've encountered this . . . It's impermanent, incapable of giving satisfaction, and subject to reversal." And in this way we come to "truly understand it." We make ourselves unhappy trying to find lasting happiness through pursuing gain, fame, praise, and pleasure. Because it can't be done. Gain, fame, praise, pleasure:

None of these things last. There's always someone who has more of them than we have, which makes us unhappy. And if we obtain them then we fear losing them. Appreciating that the worldly principles are inherently unsuitable as sources of happiness, we stop pursuing them, and feel more at ease.

I'd like to offer an example from my own life to show how practical this teaching is. I used to have powerful cravings to own the latest technology. These cravings were a source of distress. Comparing my current phone to the latest models that were on sale, it appeared dull, slow, old, and of a less impressive design. Usually it was also a bit dinged up; it had both literally and figuratively lost its luster. If I'd had lots of money, I could have just bought a new one, but alas I was only scraping by, and a nicer phone was an unaffordable luxury. Still, I was strongly tempted to spend money I didn't have on making an upgrade. That sense of wanting something and not being able to have it was a source of much dissatisfaction.

So I'd reflect that the device I already possessed was once new. I'd once longed for it in precisely the same way I now yearned for its replacement. It had once appeared lightning-fast, shiny, and the kind of thing I could impress people with. I'd recall that any new phone I bought would quickly go through the same life cycle; it wouldn't be long until it appeared dull, slow, old, and of a less impressive design than newer models. Reflecting this way, I was able to see the imperfections in the worldly principles, and my cravings diminished. The more I practiced adopting wiser perspectives, the weaker these cravings became. And the less I was bothered by yearnings for technology, the happier I was.

Tech cravings are not just about gain, but also about having the elite status of "being someone with a new phone," receiving praise ("Nice phone!"), and the pleasure of having a shiny object. All of the worldly principles can be countered in the same way, by reflecting that they're impermanent, incapable of giving satisfaction, and subject to reversal (new becomes old).

Whether we feel like meditating or not falls in the hedonistic pair of worldly principles: pleasure and pain. As we've seen, we can observe painful resistance to meditating and recognize that it's impermanent. *So what* if you don't feel good about sitting right now? That feeling won't last. Be kind to it as it passes, but don't take what it's saying seriously. Sit anyway. Think about all the other feelings you've had in your life that at one time seemed so important. Where are they now? They've all gone, like last year's snow. Seeing the impermanence of feelings, you can take your resistance less seriously. It becomes less compelling.

Reflecting that our resistance is subject to reversal, we can remind ourselves that a course of action that seems compelling now will soon seem hollow. Although skipping meditation because we don't feel like it may seem right now like a way to be happy, later we'll realize it's actually a source of disappointment.

We can't find lasting happiness within the worldly principles—by avoiding pain and pursuing what seems pleasurable, for example. But we can find lasting happiness by seeing how pointless it is to take impermanent feelings too seriously. The less driven we are by the *loka-dhammas*, the more we can embrace the *Buddha-dhamma*, doing what brings happiness in the long term rather than what seems most comfortable in the short term. And one of the best things we can do to support the arising of long-term happiness and well-being is to meditate daily.

"I meditate every day. It's just what I do. It's part of who I am. I see through the delusions inherent in the worldly principles."

Reflection

Try working through a reflection on impermanence. For example, if you're craving some material object, imagine the joy of having it as a new possession, then visualize it becoming old, becoming broken or obsolete, and then ending up in a landfill. What effect does this have on your desire? If you are hankering after some experience, remember other times you've longed for similar experiences. Where is the pleasure of them now? If they were truly satisfying, why are you craving a new experience once again?

Last Words

Watch the many ways in which the worldly winds push you first one way and then another. Develop an anchor by being aware of how impermanent your urges are, how they can't give you lasting satisfaction, and how they deliver dissatisfaction instead of the satisfaction they promise.

DAY 18

Practice in Sickness and in Health

Practice Reminder

If you meditate now, you can quiet the little inner voice that keeps asking, “Have you sat yet today?” Remember to celebrate sitting. And then record your progress. Grow that chain!

Today

A lot of people let their meditation practice slide when they get sick. But that’s a mistake. Meditating promotes healing, and it reduces the self-pity that makes being ill such a miserable experience.

Strategies

What happens to your meditation practice when you get sick? It’s tempting to take the day off, like you might do with work. Skipping work when you’re sick is sensible; you don’t want to spread an infectious disease to others, and it’s good to avoid making your illness worse by overexerting yourself. But neither of those things applies with meditation.

When Tibetan Buddhists are ill, they do *more* meditation, not less. Their reasoning is that the illness might be the result of previous bad karma, which they want to counteract with the good karma of meditation. Even if you're skeptical about that rationale, meditating while sick is still a wise move, because meditation has been shown to boost the immune system and to reduce our perception of pain and discomfort.

Although we might tell ourselves that we can't meditate while we're sick, that's not true. That's just a symptom of self-pity. Even if we feel too poorly to sit up, we can meditate lying down. Meditating lying down isn't ideal—it tends to lead to a less focused experience compared to sitting upright—but it's much better than nothing. (Please don't force yourself to sit upright in meditation if it feels like you're exhausting yourself. Practice self-kindness.)

If you have a respiratory infection, you might find that bringing attention to your breathing triggers coughing spasms, so it might work better to direct your attention elsewhere—for example, by doing loving-kindness practice. Loving-kindness is also emotionally supportive, which is handy when you're having a hard time. You can say to yourself things like "May you be well. May you be free from suffering. May you heal from this sickness. May you be at ease with discomfort." You can send kindly messages of support and encouragement to parts of the body where suffering is experienced. If your throat is sore, wish it well. If your lungs are full of mucus, wish them well. If you feel tired and achy, wish your whole body well. This is a practice of self-compassion, and it can help you support yourself through the challenge of feeling ill.

Incidentally, self-pity is not the same thing as self-compassion. Self-compassion says, "May you be well," and it reduces our suffering. Self-pity says, "Poor me, this is terrible," and increases our suffering. One time when the Buddha was sick and in great pain he was challenged by the Buddhist incarnation of doubt, Māra, who taunted him for lying around uselessly. Essentially, Māra was trying to provoke the Buddha to self-pity. The Buddha replied, "I lie down with compassion for all beings." He used his enforced rest as an opportunity to have empathy for others who are suffering. Recognizing that others are suffering too, and often much worse than we are, is a powerful antidote to self-pity. It helps us to put our own suffering in perspective. You have a sore throat, but someone else has a broken leg. You have the flu, but someone else has just learned they have cancer. If you have cancer, someone else has just lost a child to cancer. In empathizing in this way, we're counting our blessings. Our own suffering is real, but it's usually much less catastrophic than we imagine.

"I meditate every day. It's just what I do. It's part of who I am. I meditate even when I'm sick."

Going Deeper

One of the biggest misconceptions about self-compassion is that it's selfish. The term does include the word *self*, so perhaps it's not surprising that people get the wrong idea. The fact is, though, that a lack of self-compassion leads to a lack of compassion for others. If we don't know how to show compassion to ourselves, we're probably going to be too wrapped up in our own pain to be able to respond compassionately to other people. We just won't have the bandwidth available for them.

The Buddha said of the first noble truth—the fact that there is suffering in our lives—that suffering is to be *known*. We often have suffering but don't *know* it. We don't recognize it for what it is. We don't fully realize that it's happening. And because we don't know our suffering, we don't respond to it appropriately.

We get so caught up in our stories that we fail to notice the fact that we're in pain. Think about what happens when your computer is running slowly, for example. You probably think about how annoying it is, and wish the machine ran faster. You might think about whether or not you can afford a new one, or about how inept the software manufacturers are. This causes further suffering, so that we're caught up in a closed loop: suffering leads to rumination, leads to further suffering. Caught up in the story, we're unable to be kind and compassionate to ourselves. And when someone tries to engage with us at a time like this, we may well snap at them for interrupting us. We're uncompassionate.

When we know our suffering—when we recognize the fact that we're in pain or discomfort—we can drop our ruminations. We can think, "I'm frustrated right now. This frustration is a form of suffering. Maybe I should offer myself some support?" We can now turn toward to our suffering and offer it the support it needs. We can accept our pain, regarding it with kind eyes, talking to it in a soothing and supportive way, and even touching it reassuringly. Our suffering having been addressed, we've broken that closed loop. Even if the frustration is still there, we're no longer tangled up within ourselves. Our attention is more open and able to be directed outward.

No longer in such a self-obsessed state, and having awoken qualities of empathy and compassion, those qualities become available for others. We're less likely to regard them as intruding, and we're less likely to snap at them. We're more likely to meet them with empathy, recognizing that they, just like us, are feeling beings that dislike suffering and want to be at ease. And so we're more likely to be kind to them, treating them with care and respect. If we sense that they are suffering, we're more likely to show them concern and support.

Practicing self-compassion leads to compassion for others. Self-compassion is not selfish. It's what frees us from selfishness.

Reflection

Record one or two experiences of practicing self-compassion (as you did on Day 16), this time adding how your experience changed afterward—especially in relation to other people. Other things that commonly happen are the arising of a moment of clarity in which you see the painful situation you've been through in a new way, the letting go of some attitude or assumption that had been causing you pain, or the arising of compassion for others. Whatever happens, make a note of it so that you remember the value of self-compassion.

Last Words

Self-compassion is the opposite of selfishness. It's the key to living with more care and regard for others. It's self-compassion that frees us to be compassionate to others.

DAY 19

Don't Believe Everything You Think

Practice Reminder

Meditate. Celebrate. Record. You got this!

Today

We usually assume that our thoughts are true. But in fact, many of our thoughts—including thoughts that attempt to dissuade us from practicing—are inaccurate and unhelpful. It's wise to learn to recognize these unhelpful thoughts so that we can choose not to believe them.

Strategies

On Day 15 ("Outsmart Your Resistance") and Day 17 ("Don't Wait Until You Feel Like Sitting") we saw how we can become mindfully skeptical of the unpleasant feelings that accompany resistance to meditating. I'd like to talk now about how to handle the thoughts that accompany resistance.

The Buddha pointed out 2,500 years ago that our thoughts are frequently inaccurate or distorted, often to the point where they're the opposite of the truth. A pithy, modern expression of the same insight is, "Don't believe everything you think." When resistance creates a thought such as "I'm too tired and too busy to meditate today," we tend not to question it and assume it reflects reality. Rarely does it occur to us that we can question the validity of a thought, or that we could invite other thoughts that might be more accurate and helpful. But that's something we can train ourselves to do.

It would be confusing, even catastrophic, if we were to disbelieve *everything* we think, but we can remember that thoughts aren't guaranteed to be accurate and be on the lookout for those that might lead us into suffering. How do we decide which thoughts to trust? If we listen carefully to our thoughts, we'll notice that it's not always the same voice that's speaking. There's an angry voice and a loving voice, a lazy voice and an enthusiastic voice, a despondent voice and an optimistic voice, a voice that twists facts and a voice that speaks wisely—to name just a few. One thing we can do is to ask *Is this thought truly aligned with my long-term happiness and well-being?* A thought like "I can't be bothered meditating" certainly isn't. We might also find it helpful to ask *If this voice isn't wise and helpful, what other voices can I be open to hearing?*

So, when resistance says, "I'm a terrible meditator. What's the point?" or, "I missed meditation yesterday, I might as well give up," you can invite wiser and kinder voices to speak up. This isn't a matter of simply making your mind say something. It's more that you can sit with a kind, soft, accepting awareness of yourself, creating a channel for the wiser and more compassionate parts of you to offer guidance to whatever within you needs guidance. These wiser parts of us are very real. They might talk to your resistance, saying something like "I understand you're frustrated, and that's okay. May you be happy and at ease." Or they might even say just "Thanks for your input. I'll get back to you on that."

Our inner wisdom might present itself to us in the voice of another person. Usually it's someone we trust—perhaps a good friend or a teacher, who will step in and offer encouragement or reassurance. This is another of the benefits of spiritual friendship: we internalize the way another person thinks and talks, and if they're wise, then we internalize their wisdom, which then becomes part of us. For a while, though, it may still present itself as being them, and perhaps this happens because your own inner wisdom recognizes that you'll be more receptive to their voice than to one of your own.

To summarize: Rather than believing an unhelpful thought and taking it to be the only possible viewpoint you can adopt, you can be skeptical of it, and recognize it as not representing your best interests. Recognizing that it is just one voice, you can invite wiser outlooks to make themselves known. This is another strategy for dealing with resistance.

"I meditate every day. It's just what I do. It's part of who I am. And I don't believe everything I think."

Going Deeper

Henry David Thoreau commented, "Nothing was ever so unfamiliar and startling to me as my own thoughts." He was a man who undoubtedly had many unusual and creative thoughts, but really, we should be surprised by every single thought we have.

I invite you, right now, to try an experiment. It'll only take a minute or two.

First, sit quietly.

Now, ask yourself, "I wonder what my next thought is going to be?"

Then watch for a minute or two to see what happens.

If you did that little experiment, you probably found that after you asked the question there was a period where there was no inner monologue—perhaps a welcome reprieve—and then at some point, maybe all too quickly, a thought arose. The fact that it's possible to induce a pause in our thinking is interesting, especially for those of you who believe that your thinking is incessant. This probably isn't the case; more likely, you just don't notice and appreciate the pauses between bursts of thought.

Things begin to get more interesting, however, when we inquire more deeply about the thought that arose. The actual content of that thought—what it said—doesn't matter; the crucial question is, *Did you know what this thought was going to be before it appeared?*

You didn't. You simply heard the thought as it appeared, fully formed, in your mind. Are you aware of how it came to be? How was it created? How was the topic chosen? How were the words you heard put together? None of us knows. The strange thing about thoughts is we only think *we* think them. The closer we look, the clearer it is that they think themselves.

You are not the thinker. Listening to your own thoughts is like listening to someone else speaking. In both cases there are processes going on that construct speech. And you have no access to those processes. All you can detect is their outcomes: the words that arise in your mind or arrive at your ears.

When you hear thoughts, you are listening to someone talking, but it's not you. Or at least it's not the conscious you. It is obvious to anyone who has meditated that you can't get that inner voice to keep quiet for any length of time at all. Often, it chatters away whether or not you want it to. You don't choose what it says; you don't choose when it appears.

Yet although we're on the receiving end of thoughts whose origins we can know nothing about, we habitually call these thoughts ours, take them seriously, and believe most of them, especially when they say bad things about us or otherwise diminish the quality of our lives. Once we start to accept that we don't know the content of our thoughts before we hear them, and don't know how they are created, we can let ourselves be astonished by them. This is an experience of nonself. Your thoughts are not and never have been yourself. This is something we routinely choose to ignore, but there are spiritual benefits that come from allowing it into awareness.

What I'm saying here might seem strange, but it's the same thing the Buddha said. He emphasized that we are not our thoughts. He said, "Thoughts are not-self. The cause and reason that gives rise to ideas is also not-self. Since ideas are produced by what is not-self, how could they be self?"[36]

Now, I suggest you try the exercise above once again, but this time, know that you are receiving the thought rather than creating it, and see if you can let yourself be surprised. Realize that thoughts just appear. That they come from what is not you, and are not you.

We have such strong self-defenses that it's quite hard for us to be surprised by the thoughts that arise, fully formed and unbidden, in the mind. We've learned to become almost calculatedly blasé about the whole thing, in the way bored teenagers will mutter "Whatever!" and roll their eyes when something amazing is pointed out to them. Maybe it's just too weird to accept that we're constantly on the receiving end of thoughts that aren't ours. But if we can allow ourselves to be surprised by our own thoughts, it's a startling thing. We realize that we are not, as we had always assumed, our thoughts. We realize that our entire interpretation of the world of thinking has been wrong throughout our entire life.

Pema Chödrön said, "When we're having our emotional upheavals, the buddhas and bodhisattvas don't see us as stupid or hopeless; they see our confusion as mere troubled weather, ephemeral and fleeting, passing through our skylike mind."[37] Thoughts are just weather passing through. They're not part of the sky. They don't define it. Thoughts come and go all the time. Some of them are helpful, others aren't. They can be accurate or distorted. Sometimes they are selfish, sometimes selfless. They can be cruel or kind. Whatever they're like, however, none of them is ours. None of them is us. And we don't have to believe them.

Instead of credulously believing whatever thoughts bubble up from "down there"—wherever it is thoughts are formed, by whatever it is that creates them—we can pass them through the Dharmic filter of the question, "Does this support the long-term happiness of myself and others?" If they do, you can choose to treat them as valid. If they don't, you can choose to ignore them.

Reflection

Carry around the thought, "Don't believe everything you think." Let it arise randomly during the day. See if it gives you permission to choose whether or not to take your thoughts seriously.

Last Words

Who is doing the choosing or ignoring? That's a *koan* I will leave you to ponder.[38]

DAY 20

Surf Those Urges

Practice Reminder

Five minutes is all it takes to keep establishing your daily meditation practice. You can do more, of course. However long you sit, remember to celebrate and to track your progress.

Today

Urges—such as the urge to avoid meditating—can feel powerful and even overwhelming. But once we realize that they are impermanent, rising and falling like waves, we can learn to ride them out without acting on them.

Strategies

Alan Marlatt, a professor of psychology who developed the Mindfulness-Based Relapse Prevention (MBRP) treatment program, came up with the term "urge surfing" to describe how mindfulness can help us deal with cravings. Although his work involved helping people to quit alcohol, heroin, and other addictive substances, it also applies to us as we work on developing the habit of meditating daily. Yes, we're talking about feelings and resistance yet again. We are approaching this topic from many angles. Just as you might hit a rock with a hammer, we keep trying until we split the thing open.

From time to time the desire to meditate is bound come into conflict with the urge not to meditate. This may happen when you think about meditating, or it may happen while you're in the middle of a sit. Now, emotions are like ocean waves—large and powerful. Your rational brain is more like someone who's in the ocean: small and weak in comparison to the waves. Your rational brain can't stop the waves, but it can learn to ride them, using mindfulness as a surfboard.

To help you practice urge surfing, see if you can remember, in vivid detail, what it's like to have a strong aversion to sitting down to meditate, or the urge to stop and to walk away from your cushion. Really feel it.

Now, identify where the feeling is most prominently located in the body. Recognize it as just another sensation. Notice how it rises and falls in intensity, over and over. It'll tend to intensify as certain thoughts appear. And it'll weaken as those thoughts naturally pass away.

You may well fear that the urge will keep getting stronger and stronger. But know that that's not how emotions work. Emotions are like waves. They rise and fall. Know that if you ride it out, the urge will crest like a wave, diminish, and eventually vanish.

Above all, remember that although your urges, like waves, will pass, you will remain. And so will your commitment to practice.

There will be times when you fall off the surfboard of mindfulness and find yourself struggling to scramble back aboard, but this is how you gain skill in surfing. You gain the confidence that you can ride out your waves of discomfort and resistance and remain true to your deeper values and long-term goals.

In time you start to realize something interesting. Your urges present themselves as imperatives. They give the impression they must be obeyed. But after they've subsided it seems doubtful that they had any validity at all. Keep observing this, and you come to see that urges seem irresistible only because you believe they are. Lose that belief, and they lose their power.

"I meditate every day. It's just what I do. It's part of who I am. I surf waves of resistance until they pass."

Going Deeper

Understanding that things change, or are impermanent or unstable (*anicca*), is undoubtedly the most important practice in the entire Buddhist tradition. Impermanence is not something that can be understood easily. Yes, it's easy to intellectually understand the meaning of the words "Everything is impermanent. Everything comes to an end." But we're aiming at a deeper, more experiential understanding of this principle. It's an understanding that can come about only gradually, through hard and sometimes painful work. Working out its full implications can take a lifetime, or (they say) even longer.

We can understand impermanence on many levels. The Buddha talked about the universe in its totality being impermanent, with great cycles lasting billions of years. In each of these cycles, the material world grows and evolves, only to collapse and start over again. This cycle, according to ancient Indian cosmology, would continue endlessly: cycle after cycle after cycle.

The Buddha said, "There comes a time when the great earth is burned up and destroyed, and is no more."[39] Science tells us this won't happen for billions of years, and our minds tend to equate "being around longer than me" with "lasts forever." We might look at a mountain and think it's permanent and unchanging, but of course it's not: Open a geology textbook and you'll see that when viewed in a larger timescale, the mountain is like a ripple on a pond. Everything that's come into being changes. Everything comes to an end.

On a more intimate timescale, human lives begin and end. We know this, although we often prefer not to think about it. Knowing this, the Buddha suggested that each of us should reflect on the fact that we are prone to aging, getting sick, dying, and being separated from everything we cherish. And in light of that he asked us to reflect that we're responsible for our lives. We could boil this question down to a more vernacular one: "I'm not here long; what's the best use of my time? What's the best way for me to relate to others in the brief time that I'm with them?" These reflections lead to us seeing life as a precious opportunity to find joy, meaning, and love. (This is something we'll return to on Day 26: Find Your Deeper "Why.")

More intimately still, thoughts, feelings, urges, and sensations all begin and end. This is something that we sometimes need to struggle with before we can accept it. It's surprisingly common that when we find ourselves unhappy, we fear that this state will go on forever. This mistaken perception adds immeasurably to our suffering: It turns feeling blue into depression, and anxiety into panic and desperation. This assumption that we're stuck with our feelings can happen when we find ourselves happy, too, and this leads inevitably to disappointment when some emotional shift brings our joy to an end.

It can be enormously helpful to remind ourselves that a particular feeling or emotion is going to end. I've had times when I've been intensely worried about something. In the midst of those experiences I've remembered previous times I've been worried. I've then asked myself, "Where are those feelings now? Where are the feelings of the past?" Remembering that they have long gone has helped me appreciate that whatever I'm going through right now will also pass. I just have to ride it out. The same is true for any other painful experience, such as sadness, loneliness, or longing.

We can go deeper yet into the experience of impermanence. Whatever feeling or sensation we care to examine, whether it's pain, or pressure, or coolness, it is not one solid, unchanging thing. Any complex sensation involves thousands, or hundreds of thousands, of nerve endings. And these nerve endings are not continuously active, but fire on and off rapidly. If we allow the mind to become settled enough to look closely at the texture of a sensation, we can see that it's ever-changing. It has a twinkling, shimmering quality, as nerve endings, distributed through the three-dimensional space of the body, fire and rest, fire and rest. We realize that this experience is not a thing, but an ever-changing process. It's not even that there is a thing that changes. Take away the change, and there is no "thing" left. Everything is a process of becoming, empty of being.

When we examine experiences in this way, we may start to see them very differently from before. Pain can cease to be painful. Anxiety may cease to be scary. Desire may become hollow and unconvincing. Sadness just evaporates. Feelings that were painful one moment can transform into energy and bliss. Seeing the impermanence of urges that do not support our long-term happiness and well-being, we no longer need to follow through on them. The more we experience ourselves as changing, moment by moment, the freer we become.

Reflection

From time to time, take one sensation that seems relatively solid and stable, and examine it closely. See if you can observe whether this moment right now is different from the moment just before. How about this moment? And this one? And this one?

Last Words

Everything changes. Nothing is here for long, including ourselves. The more we bear that in mind, the more appreciative we will be for opportunities to practice.

DAY 21

Remember You're Fallible

Practice Reminder

Remember: Sit. Celebrate! Record your progress. And keep repeating the mantra: "I meditate every day. It's just what I do. It's part of who I am."

Today

Be on your guard: A run of success can make you cocky; cockiness can lead to you neglecting to do the things that led to your success; and no longer doing those things inevitably leads to you slipping up.

Strategies

Imagine that some neighbors who are also dear friends had asked you to go round to their house every day to feed their cat while they were away on a two-week vacation. But then, on the day they are due to return, you realize with horror that you'd completely forgotten to do the task that had been asked of you. In the entire time your friends have been gone, you haven't fed the cat even once! It's been in the house all on its own. Is it even alive?

That's how sick I felt when, after months of daily practice, I missed a day of meditation. I'm not exaggerating. I felt like I had let something precious die. I felt mortified. I felt I had let myself and others down. I thought I should give up.

What happened was this: At that time my children were still very young, and every day I faced the chaos and disruptions to daily schedules typical of that phase of their lives. I'd intended to meditate last thing at night, because I'd been busy all day, switching off between work and childcare. But I was exhausted, and I forgot to sit, and as soon as my head hit the pillow, I was asleep. When I awoke in the morning I realized what had happened. I'd broken my perfect run, and the situation wasn't fixable. It was too late.

I recount this for you because it might happen that you, too, will have a long run of success, and that you too will have a slip, feel desperately bad about it, and feel like you should give up making the effort. Missing a day early on is a different story. As I've already pointed out, it's natural that when we're first establishing a habit, we'll have slip-ups. After all, we're still working at putting into place the strategies that will eventually help us succeed. You break a run of five days or even twenty-five days, and you can shrug and start again. When you've built up a run of 125 or 225 days, the stakes seem higher. In my case my failure was, paradoxically, due to my success. Having meditated every day for months, I believed I'd cracked the secret of meditating without fail. I'd become cocky and complacent. I lost my sense of fallibility.

I've noticed that this happens in other areas of my life as well. Sometimes I've followed a particular recipe several times, and that meal turns out consistently delicious. But then I get sloppy. I forget that my success has been due to combining certain ingredients in a certain way. The meal becomes disappointingly over-seasoned, under-seasoned, or just not tasty, and I can't understand why until I look back at the recipe and see that I've omitted some key step, missed an ingredient, or haven't measured things properly.

In the case of my meditation slip-up, I'd assumed that because I'd been successful in the past, I'd continue to be successful in the future. I forgot the part about needing to do the things that had brought success in the first place. For example, I'd forgotten to create either a plan A or a plan B, and I'd stopped repeating the "I meditate every day" mantra. I'd forgotten about the principle of conditionality: that for something to arise the appropriate conditions must first exist.

And so the thought came into my head, "I've failed. I can't do this. I'll just give up. I've broken my streak." Worst of all, I thought, "I can no longer say that I meditate every day. After all, I missed a day!" But here's something: You brush your teeth every day. It's just what you do. It's part of who you are. But if for some reason you were unable to brush your teeth for twenty-four hours—let's say you're on a flight to the other side of the planet and your carry-on bag had mysteriously vanished—you wouldn't say, "OK, that's it! I'm going to give up brushing my teeth daily." That's not what being a Rock-Solid Daily Tooth-Brusher means. You'd just shrug and brush your teeth again as soon as you could. So when you make a big slip with your meditation practice, just get straight back to your daily practice as soon as you can. It's not really as big a deal as you thought.

It did, however, seem like a big deal at the time. Fortunately, I didn't buy in to the "just give up" story I'd been telling myself. I kept going with my practice. But I realized that I had some forgiveness to do, and so I laid a hand on my solar plexus, where the pain of forgetting was most prominent, and told myself over and over again that it was OK to make mistakes, that it was OK to forget to meditate sometimes, that it was hard to develop a new habit, that I was a work-in-progress, that my happiness didn't depend on my being perfect, but on my being kind to myself, and that my "imperfect" run of meditations was actually an achievement to be proud of, especially given how complicated my life was.

Practicing self-forgiveness and self-compassion in this way didn't make my disappointment and embarrassment magically disappear. But it did make them easier to live with until they naturally subsided. And practicing self-compassion stopped me from giving up in disgust. It seems that I miss a day every two years or so. I don't like that it happens, but it isn't such a big deal, and I no longer get upset when it happens.

Sometimes we fear that self-forgiveness and self-compassion will set us up to fail, and that we need to be tough on ourselves to succeed. But it's the opposite that's true. It's when we beat ourselves up that we want to give up. The reality is that we are not infallible. We are all going to slip up. Remembering this keeps us watchful. It arouses *appamāda*, or diligence, which maintains the strategies that keep us meditating every day. And when we do slip up, self-forgiveness makes it easier for us to pick ourselves up again and keep going. To err is inevitable. To forgive oneself is divine.

"I meditate every day. It's just what I do. It's part of who I am. When I slip up, I forgive myself and get straight back to practicing."

Going Deeper

Isaac of Nineveh, an important figure in the seventh-century Christian Church, wrote, "Blessed is the man who knows his own weakness, because this knowledge becomes to him the foundation, root and beginning of all goodness."[40] These words are an excellent reminder of the importance of humility.

Humility is where we're open about our weaknesses. The Buddha encouraged us to be as honest as we possibly can be about our failings. In a discussion with his son, Rahula, he said that we should reflect on our actions, thoughts, and speech before, while, and after doing them.[41] We should ask whether these acts "lead to hurting myself, hurting others, or hurting both." We should also ask ourselves whether they're "unskillful, with suffering as [their] outcome and result." If our actions are harmful to ourselves or others, or are unskillful, we're urged to stop (if it's something we're currently doing), not do it (if it's something we were planning on doing), and to "confess, reveal, and clarify such a deed to a wise person or a fellow spiritual practitioner" if it's something we've already done. Naturally, if our self-reflections indicate that no one (not even ourselves) will be hurt and we're not motivated by unskillful intentions, we're urged to carry on and to be pleased by our actions, as we "train day and night in skillful qualities."

The Buddha is advocating the practice of humility. Humility is not us saying we are lowly or lesser. It's us saying, "This is what I am working with. These are my mistakes, and here's what I'm doing about them." Humility involves self-awareness and self-scrutiny, because we need to know what our weaknesses are before we can admit to them. It requires honesty, in the form of a willingness to be open to others about who we are. And it requires trust and courage: knowing that it's OK to reveal our weaknesses to ourselves and to others. If we lack humility, we will refuse to acknowledge our shortcomings and therefore find it almost impossible to change.

Confession and apology are powerful practices. Apologizing is something you're familiar with and hopefully are comfortable doing. Sometimes people think apologizing is a sign of weakness, but it's not. It's a sign of fearlessness. If you're reluctant to offer apologies, take a deep breath and plunge in. It gets easier with practice, until you almost feel it's imperative to apologize when you've done something hurtful or deceitful. You recognize you've caused a rift between yourself and another person, and you take responsibility for repairing the damaged relationship as best you can. You want to restore trust, if possible. You want to let anyone you've hurt or let down know that they matter.

If apologizing can sometimes be daunting, confessing can be even more so. The first time I confessed in a formal setting, I was deeply afraid that my fellow practitioners would see me as a horrible person, dislike me, and even shun me. That didn't happen. There was a little ritual of acknowledgment at the end, with everyone taking turns saying

"I hear and accept your confession. May you be purified." As each person said these words, they looked me in the eyes, not with rejection, but with pure love and acceptance. I felt fully accepted as I was, a bundle of skillful and unskillful tendencies working, falteringly, to purify itself. And when it was my turn to accept others' confessions I was full of admiration for the way their particular ecosystems of emotional qualities were working to become happier and more helpful to the world.

It's important that those to whom we open up about our shortcomings, and about what we're struggling with in our practice, be capable of receiving such a gift. The Buddha suggested "teachers and fellow practitioners" as suitable recipients for our confessions and admissions. A person who is not doing the same work we are engaged with might either use what we say against us or encourage us to continue acting unskillfully, since to them it might be no big deal. In order for us to be vulnerable with others we need to build connections of deep trust and mutual respect with them. But we build those connections precisely through expressing our vulnerability. The key is mutuality; spiritual friends and community expressing a shared vulnerability that deepens the growth of all involved.

One of the most life-changing lessons I've learned is that concealing our faults creates a barrier between ourselves and others, while humbly admitting our shortcomings connects us with other spiritual practitioners in shared vulnerability and intimacy.

Reflection

Notice when others share their struggles and reveal the difficult stuff it is they're working on. Respect what they're doing, and express that respect to them. Let yourself recognize your own complexity and the messiness of your spiritual practice, and see if you can be open and vulnerable, sharing the work you're doing. These exchanges build trust and respect.

Last Words

Being honest with ourselves about our weaknesses makes us stronger. Being honest with others about our weaknesses creates trust, making our connections with them stronger.

DAY 22

Learn to Sit with Pain

Practice Reminder

You can do this! Keep sitting, even if it's just for five minutes. And remember to celebrate and to record your practice.

Today

The physical discomfort caused by injury, aging, or just from sitting still can make us want to avoid meditating. With practice, however, we can learn to be more at ease with discomfort.

Strategies

We've already talked about how we can keep meditating daily even during times of illness, but it's worth discussing physical pain and discomfort separately; we can be ill but not in pain, or in pain but not ill. When we have either chronic or short-term pain it can be hard to bring ourselves to meditate, because doing so brings to the center of our attention something that we'd rather not be experiencing at all. Because of this, it can seem at first that meditating makes our pain more intense.

Many studies, however, have shown that meditating ultimately reduces pain. Even novice meditators begin to process pain differently from the average nonmeditator, so that they find pain less painful. A part of the brain called the ventromedial prefrontal cortex becomes less active when meditators experience pain. This brain region plays a key role in self-narrative, which includes us talking to ourselves about our experience. In short, meditators are telling themselves fewer stories, like "This is horrible. I can't stand it. I wish this would stop." The ventromedial prefrontal cortex is second-arrow central. When it's less active, we fire fewer second arrows at ourselves, and so we suffer less.

Meditators also learn to treat pain as less of a personal threat by training themselves to regard pain and discomfort as sensations they're observing rather than immersed in. Normally we experience pain as if we are, as the Buddha put it, "conjoined with it,"[42] and so our stance is that "we" are suffering. It's as if we imagine ourselves *within* the pain, or fused with it. Indeed, we often say "I'm *in* pain." But when we take up the stance of mindful observing, pain becomes an object in relation to us. There are now sensations of pain *there* and an aware observer *here*. Mentally there is a gap between us and the pain. We are no longer in it, and this shift of perception means that the pain is less alarming. These are simple yet practical applications of the teaching of nonself.

Another reason meditators are less troubled by pain is that their brains learn to process pain signals differently, treating them more like ordinary sensations such as touch, temperature, and so on. This comes about because meditating makes a part of the brain called the thalamus less active. The thalamus seems to act as a kind of "switchboard" in the brain, and it can learn to screen out some of the sensations of pain.[43] Meditators learn to accept pain rather than to resist it. Paradoxically, accepting pain reduces it, while resistance (the second arrow) increases it.[44] So even though the prospect of meditating when you have a bad back or a headache might not be a pleasant one, meditating can help reduce your discomfort. It has to be said, however, that this takes a little practice.

Over the years I've been meditating I've had many opportunities to learn to sit with pain, from sore knees and backaches to full-blown migraines. If you have pain, whether chronic or short-term, what I suggest is this:

- Regard pain as just another sensation to be mindful of. It's no different from the pressure of your knees on the floor, the touch of air in your airways, or the movements of the chest and belly. It's just one more thing to observe.
- Notice that the mind's storytelling about pain is unhelpful. Keep letting go of those thoughts, turning your attention instead back to the physical sensations arising from the body. One of the stories we tell ourselves is that we need to get rid of the pain. We don't. The aim is to accept and investigate pain.
- If you need to, offer yourself emotional reassurance as you observe painful sensations. You can say to yourself, "It's OK to feel this. Let me feel this. You can do it. You're OK. You're doing great."
- Breathe with your discomfort. Often we tense up around pain and prevent the body moving the way it should. Notice any physical movements of the breathing that are taking place in the part of the body that's hurting, and let them happen. For example, the spine naturally lengthens on every in-breath and settles downward on every out-breath. Tensing inhibits this, causing further pain; softening allows the body to move again, reducing pain.
- If the pain is in a part of the body that's not obviously moving with the breathing, imagine the breath flowing through the body, within and around the area of discomfort. For example, if your knees are sore, you can imagine the breath is being drawn up from the earth and through your legs as you breathe in, and flowing back down through your legs as you breathe out.
- Investigate the pain to see what it is made of. The label "pain" suggests that we're noticing a monolithic thing, but in fact the

experience of pain is made up of many smaller sensations, such as tingling, pulsing, throbbing, heat, cold, pressure, and so on. Which sensation is prominent in any given moment changes. It's easier to sit with many small sensations than one large one.

- Each of these smaller "sub-sensations," is constantly changing, rising and falling in waves, so that what you're observing isn't the same from one moment to the next. Similar to the practice of "urge surfing," we can ride out each of these rising and falling waves. Using a technique called "noting," you can mentally name the most prominent sensations as they come in and out of focus. One moment the most prominent sensation may be pressure, and so you can say, "pressure, pressure" to yourself. The next moment you might note "heat, heat." The next moment, "tingling, tingling." Other sensations we might note are pulsing, throbbing, sharpness, and cold. The act of naming helps keep a little distance between us and the pain, so that we're less conjoined with it.
- Notice gaps in the pain. Sometimes, even if just for moments, the pain may stop being painful. Appreciate this, but don't try to hold on to it, to make it happen, or mourn when these moments pass.
- Love your pain. Pain is the feeling of your body trying to heal itself for you. It needs your support, not your aversion. Regard it with kind eyes. Offer it words of gratitude and support.
- The single most important thing about sitting with pain is not to try to get rid of it. Just be with it, accept it, and investigate it with curiosity.

You're training yourself to notice pain's component sensations; you're not focusing on the whole, but on things that are smaller and constantly changing. The more curious your mind can be about these, the less it reacts with aversion. The more you notice these sub-sensations rising and falling, the less solid the discomfort seems to be. There's less there to react to.

Another approach to sitting with pain is to bring your attention to whatever isn't painful. Some of the worst pain I've had has been with migraine headaches. It took me a long time to learn to meditate with these. At first, consciously paying attention to the symptoms of the migraine—especially the nausea—made them more intense. I needed a new approach. Eventually I started observing everything that *wasn't* pain and nausea. For example, I might find that despite all the unpleasant things going on in my body, there was a pleasurable tingling in my calf muscles. And paying attention to that sensation encouraged it to spread, surrounding and outweighing the discomfort of the migraine. This wasn't an attempt to avoid experiencing the pounding headache and waves of nausea. It wasn't aversion. It was an attempt to see these things in a more balanced way: Yes, those unpleasant things were there, but so were others that were pleasant or even just neutral. Noticing whatever is not pain creates a more balanced experience.

Practicing in this way, I found it much easier to observe my pain and nausea with acceptance and curiosity. Even if the pain was intense, it was more manageable, and sometimes the intensity of the migraine would diminish. From having been a crippling pain, it could fade to the point where it was easier to ignore, and I could meditate and then go about my day untroubled.

Although it's natural to be afraid of pain and to want to avoid it, I'd encourage you to do the opposite: "Turn toward the fire, and enter, confident," to quote Dante. Pain need not deter you from practicing meditation. Meditating will help you be more at peace with pain, which will help you in your meditation practice and in your life as a whole.

"I meditate every day. It's just what I do. It's part of who I am. Nothing, not even pain, is an obstacle."

Going Deeper

Early Buddhist teachings discuss three kinds of pain. First there's "the pain that's simply pain" (*dukkha-dukkhatā*). Then there's the suffering that we create for ourselves by resistance (*sankhara-dukkhatā*). And finally there's the suffering that comes from trying to distract ourselves from pain, often by numbing it (*vipariṇāma-dukkhatā*). It's important to understand these so that we can learn how not to bring unnecessary suffering into our lives.

The Pain That's Simply Pain

They say that pain is inevitable, but suffering is optional. This isn't strictly a Buddhist aphorism, but it's very much in line with the Buddha's teaching.

Ordinary physical pain is indeed an inevitable part of life. No matter how careful we are, the body will get injured. It'll get sick, giving rise to physical discomfort. And as it ages it'll become stiffer and sorer. This is *dukkha-dukkhatā* (the pain that's pain), or primary pain.

We also experience many painful feelings (*vedanas*), such as anxiety, frustration, grief, and hurt. Although we consider these mental phenomena, they're primarily experienced in the body. We tend to notice painful feelings in the midline of the body: around the heart, the diaphragm, and the gut. Just like ordinary physical pain, painful feelings are inevitable, and I consider them to be in the same category as *dukkha-dukkhatā*.

The Pain That Comes from Resistance

It's hardly surprising that we don't like to experience physical pain or painful feelings; their entire purpose is to warn us of potential harms, and if pain wasn't unpleasant it wouldn't get our attention and so it wouldn't be evolutionarily helpful. There's a reason we don't design fire alarms to have pleasant, reassuring sounds. Like a fire alarm, pain insists upon being noticed, precisely to motivate us to take steps to avoid harm.

Because we dislike pain, we often respond to it with mental aversion in the form of self-pity, resistance, and complaining. We might have thoughts along the lines of "This is horrible. Why is this happening? I wish it would stop. No one cares!" We want it to be gone. We might also tense the body around it, as if we're bracing against the pain, trying to wall it off or to physically push it away. These acts of aversion create a whole new layer of physical and emotional pain, and that's what the pain of resistance is. It's pain we create for ourselves. It's pain we fabricate. The word for "fabricating" in Pali is *sankhara*, and so this is *sankhara-dukkhatā*, the pain we create for ourselves. In the saying, "Pain is inevitable; suffering is optional," created pain is the optional part. We don't *have* to resist; doing so is just a strong habit. With a little mindfulness, we can learn to recognize that our resistance to pain is only creating more pain.

The Buddha described the first form of pain (*dukkha-dukkhatā*) as being like an arrow we've been shot with. He said that the second form of suffering, the pain we create for ourselves through resistance, is like a second arrow. It's as if we're responding to being shot by an arrow by firing yet another arrow at ourselves.

The Pain That Comes from Avoidance

The Buddha talked about a third response to our initial pain. This time, instead of resisting pain, we try to escape it by chasing pleasure instead.

It's not that we necessarily get to *experience* the pleasure we're seeking. Often, we don't. However, the pursuit of pleasure is itself a distraction from our pain. To escape discomfort—and it's usually emotional rather than physical discomfort—we might fantasize about doing something nice. We do this in meditation sometimes; it's the hindrance of sense-desire. We might even go and do something we find pleasurable. For example, we get bored at work, and we check social media. We're upset, and we eat our feelings, so to speak. We also sometimes use pleasurable activities as a way to avoid meditating.

Avoidance isn't a successful strategy for dealing with pain. In many cases the problem we were avoiding is still waiting for us at the end of our period of distractedness, just as unpleasant as it was before, and perhaps even more so. Also, the pleasurable activities we distract ourselves with tend not to be healthy. In the pursuit of pleasure we eat too much, eat unhealthily, drink too much, or spend too much time on social media. At the end we're left feeling disappointed with or even disgusted with ourselves.

The Buddha called this form of suffering *vipariṇāma-dukkhatā*, or the pain of reversal. We've tried to run away from our suffering, only to discover that we're pulled back into it again. The Buddha didn't offer an arrow analogy to go with this form of suffering, but you could think of it as an arrow dipped into a narcotic drug that's intended to numb your suffering; once it wears off you still have pain of the original wound, plus a hangover.

Ways to Deal with Suffering

The Buddha's teachings offer us ways to suffer less. We need to accept the primary pain of the first arrow, and drop both the reactive, ruminative thinking of the second arrow and the grasping, pleasure-seeking thinking of the third arrow.

Usually by the time any discomfort has arisen we've already begun reacting. If, for example we become restless while we're meditating, we'll find that we have second-arrow thoughts like "How long until it's over? I can't do this!" Or we'll have third-arrow thoughts about the pleasant things we'd rather be doing.

Whether we have aversive thoughts or grasping ones, we can recognize that we're reacting, and that these things are not only not helping, but are making things worse. Without blame, we simply let go of these thoughts. And when we do so, we stop stabbing ourselves with the second and third arrows.

Having done this, the key is now to accept our initial discomfort—the pain of the first arrow. We can notice the actual physical discomfort of this in the body. We might notice an uncomfortable feeling of restlessness in the arms and legs. Maybe there's a general jitteriness in the body. Perhaps there's a constricted feeling around the heart. Observe those sensations. Tell yourself it's OK to be experiencing these things. Allow them to be there. Breathe with them. Accept their discomfort as being a sensation like any other. Talk to them kindly. What we find is that without second-arrow resistance or third-arrow avoidance, our initial pain becomes more manageable. It might actually turn out to be much milder than we'd expected; our second- and third-arrow responses to suffering are usually massive overreactions.

So we sit, we experience discomfort, we continue sitting.

I don't mean to imply this this is easy to learn. We are talking about working with deeply entrenched habits of resistance, and those habits can be hard to change. But once we know that sitting with discomfort is possible, and know the steps involved, we have something we can work at and get better at. And the more we practice, the easier it is to avoid suffering, and to sit with pain.

Reflection

Notice examples of the first, second, and third arrows of pain and suffering in your own life. Bear in mind that these may overlap and coexist. Practice accepting your discomfort, letting go of the ruminative thinking that exacerbates your suffering, and find healthier alternatives to pleasure-chasing avoidance strategies.

Last Words

The Buddha didn't categorize the various ways we suffer because it's cool to know stuff. He did it because it's useful. Learn it so you can recognize it in action and work with it to free yourself from unnecessary suffering.

DAY 23

Incubate Your Potential

Practice Reminder

If you haven't sat already you can take care of that right now. You don't need perfect conditions. You don't need to be in a special place. Just sit, for five minutes at least. Then congratulate yourself and record your progress.

Today

By now we've learned many strategies for encouraging the arising of a Rock-Solid Daily Meditation Practice. Before you read the following, see how many of those strategies you can recall. Try counting them in your head or writing them down.

Strategies

The Buddha offered a lovely illustration of how the use of practical strategies brings about positive change—even in the absence of willpower.

> *Suppose there was a hen with eight, ten, or twelve eggs that she had covered, incubated, and nurtured properly. Even though no such wish as this might arise in her: "Oh, that my chicks might pierce their shells with the points of their claws and beaks and hatch safely!" Yet the chicks are capable of piercing their shells with the points of their*

claws and beaks and of hatching safely. For what reason? Because that hen with eight, ten, or twelve eggs had covered, incubated, and nurtured them properly.[45]

The hen has a collection of strategies, including covering, incubating, and nurturing her eggs. She doesn't try to force anything to happen. All she needs to do is keep applying those strategies, and her chicks will hatch. She doesn't make anything happen. She has no need of willpower.

To establish a Rock-Solid Daily Meditation Habit, what we need is a battery of strategies. Those nurture our practice, setting up the conditions for daily practice to arise. The strategies we've learned so far include:

1. Creating a visual tracking system and not breaking the chain.
2. Starting with small, manageable steps, such as five-minute meditations.
3. Planning when, where, how, and for how long you'll meditate.
4. Creating contingency plans for when things don't go as expected.
5. Celebrating, as a reward for meditating.
6. Changing your self-view by use of the mantra "I meditate every day. It's just what I do. It's part of who I am."
7. Keeping ourselves accountable by tracking our progress on apps, sharing it with other people, or engaging in self-blackmail.
8. Anchoring new habits to old ones.
9. Celebrating the freedom found in moments of mindfulness.
10. Finding enjoyment in our practice.
11. Feeling the sense of connection that comes from meditating with others, or even just listening to guided meditations.

12. Regarding every meditation as a good meditation.
13. Changing your mindset so that you see learning a new habit as an adventure.
14. Developing a growth mindset.
15. Bringing more ritual into the time before and after your meditation practice.
16. Having a special place to meditate, and making it both meaningful and beautiful.
17. Turning your obstacles into allies by becoming mindful of your resistance.
18. Having empathy for the future you.
19. Practicing self-compassion when our practice becomes difficult.
20. Being skeptical of our feelings of resistance.
21. Not seeing illness as an excuse to stop practicing, but as a reason to continue.
22. Not believing everything you think, especially if the thoughts are about not meditating.
23. Urge-surfing: being aware of the impermanence of our resistance.
24. Learning to look closely at pain, so that we reduce our resistance to it.
25. Practicing self-forgiveness when we slip up.

That's a lot of strategies that we can use, and there are more to come!

I suggest that another strategy we could add to that list is "Remembering the strategies that you already know."

The word *sati*, for mindfulness, originally meant "memory." This is curious, because memory is about the past, and usually mindfulness is about noticing what's happening right now, in the present. So what's the connection between memory and being aware of the present moment? As anyone who's practiced mindfulness knows, the most difficult thing is to remember to do it. We keep forgetting to be mindful. *Sati*, as "remembering," is *remembering to be present*.

We've seen that sati and sampajañña (intentionality) are closely associated in the Buddha's teachings. We need to remember not just to be present, but also to remember our intentions. And if our intention is to meditate daily, we need to have memorized the strategies that allow us to do that. Only if we've committed to memory the various tools and strategies we've experimented with are they available for us to use. The more strategies we've remembered, the stronger is our ability to stay true to our intention. We use these strategies to incubate our potential, in the same way a mother hen sits on her eggs until they hatch.

"I meditate every day. It's just what I do. It's part of who I am. I remember the tools that keep me on track."

Going Deeper

In the Buddha's day, spiritual teachings were never written down but were passed on by word of mouth. Writing would have been used only for mundane matters such as business agreements and receipts. Spiritual matters were considered far too important to be committed to writing for a number of reasons. First, India was a place where extreme heat, rain, humidity, or small rodents and insects could easily destroy an entire library in one unfortunate event. Second, the ancients believed that if we began to rely on books and scrolls as a repository of knowledge, our understanding of that knowledge would be weakened. The proper and safe place to store important information was in the mind.

During the Buddha's lifetime there were monks whose job it was to preserve the teachings. They were walking libraries, and this was a full-time job. The memorizers of the texts would recite the texts in unison to make sure that they were memorized accurately. If someone made an error during the chanting they'd immediately be aware they were saying something different from everyone else. These monks didn't meditate! They didn't have the time. Meditating was another specialized task carried out by another subgroup of the monastic community. Although these two functions were meant to be complementary, there were sometimes tensions and rivalries between these two monastic groups.[46]

The oral nature of the Buddhist scriptures can be seen in the vast number of lists and sublists they contain: This was a way of making it easier to commit them to memory. It can also be seen in the often mind-numbing repetition of the early scriptures, where entire lengthy paragraphs are repeated verbatim, sometimes with just one word changed.

It's worth us asking ourselves how much of the teachings we have at our fingertips. We might recognize the teachings when we see them, but not be able to recall them at will. Can we recite even the four noble truths, let alone the eightfold path or the twelve links of conditionality? Knowing these by heart makes it far easier for us to reflect on them. Often the best times for reflection are not those where we sit ourselves in front of a book, when the mind can be overly focused and not amenable to making creative connections. The best times for reflection are when we're relaxed and the mind is calm and mindful, tethered by mindfulness but able to float lightly and to make creative connections between one teaching and another, between the teachings and our lives. This kind of creative investigation is more difficult to do if we can remember only three of the noble truths and six factors of the eightfold path, and if we aren't clear on their order.

I feel fortunate, because at the Dharma center I attended early on, we were encouraged to memorize key Buddhist teachings. Our teachers had noticed that people were struggling to make sense of half-remembered teachings, and began urging us to take memorization seriously. So for a few weeks, rather than simply having our usual free-flowing discussions about the implications of the Buddha's teachings, we memorized lists together. We recited them. We tested ourselves and each other. We practiced recalling them forward and in reverse order. Sometimes we memorized them in Pali as well as in English. This memorization practice had a powerful effect on many of us who participated in these sessions. It became easier when we were studying one topic to make connections with another. We felt more confident in our grasp of what the Buddha taught.

Suggesting that you be able to recall the many tools we've been learning in this book is an extension of that same practice of Dharma memorization. When we find ourselves floundering, unsure, anxious, confused, or doubting ourselves, it's enormously helpful to be able to say, "Oh, yes! I can do *this*, or *this*, or *this*." It gives us confidence. We know there's something we can do to help us overcome forgetfulness and resistance, and establish skillful habits.

If we can't recall the strategies we've been experimenting with, we may feel hopeless. So please spend a little time committing to memory the tools I've listed above. The more of them you can remember, the more tools you'll have to draw upon in times of crisis.

Reflection

If we don't remember that we have tools available to us, they're not of much use. So see if you can find ways to commit them to memory. Use as many senses as possible as you do this. For example, instead of merely reminding yourself of the words "Create a visual tracking system," visualize yourself putting a big check mark on a calendar, feeling the marker in your hand, smelling the scent of the solvents, and even hearing the point of the marker as it runs against the paper.

Last Words

Remembering Dharma teachings and the principles behind them brings confidence.

DAY 24

Find Your Edge

Practice Reminder

Sit. Celebrate. Record your progress. And then celebrate the effort you're putting into developing the habit of sitting daily. Even if you've missed days, you can still celebrate—in fact it's especially important!

Today

When we let our practice stagnate it's no longer really practice, in the sense that we're no longer consciously working on developing skills. When this happens, our meditation becomes habitual and mechanical, and we lose our enthusiasm for it. So it's helpful to remember that meditation is about developing skills, and to work on developing those skills. When we do that our meditation—our *practice*—can remain a source of fascination.

Strategies

We use the word *practice* as a synonym for meditating—"How's your practice going?"—but sometimes we don't bear in mind its true meaning. Practicing means working with the conscious intent to improve a skill. Is that what we're actually doing when we're meditating?

The Buddha compared meditating with the development of other skills such as archery. He said that an archer would practice their craft repeatedly, learning how to shoot long distances, to shoot rapidly, and to pierce the target more deeply. Similarly, a meditator should train to sustain attention, observe moments as they pass rapidly by, and closely examine the nature of thoughts, feelings, and sensations. I'd encourage you to approach meditation in that spirit by having in mind something that you're consciously working on. Seeing the purpose of your meditation as being to deepen skills, you can ask, "Where's my edge in this sit?"

As an example, say you want to work on cultivating sustained attention, so that periods of distractedness happen less often. (This is akin to an archer practicing shooting arrows long distances.) With the form of mindfulness of breathing I most often teach, we settle the mind by counting breaths in cycles of ten. You'll usually find when you do this that in any given sit you reliably get distracted after a certain number of breaths. Some days you keep getting distracted after just three breaths, while other days it might be after thirty. Knowing this, you can be more vigilant as you're approaching the distraction zone, wherever that may happen to lie on a particular day. As you near the point where distraction keeps arising, you can make more effort to be attentive and see if you can keep your attention steady. This can help you get through the distraction zone with your mindfulness intact, and so you extend the length of time that you're able to be mindful. This is rewarding, which is what happens when your meditation practice actually is practice.

That is just one example of where you can look for an edge to work on. You could also work on being more aware of the kinds of thoughts that distract you: Are they to do with fantasizing about pleasure, with conflict, with worrying, with doubting yourself, or with dreaminess? Understanding this can help you to overcome the specific kind of distraction that's afflicting you. For example, if your thoughts are angry ones, you can look for some kindness for yourself and others. And if you want to bring more kindness into your practice, you can keep asking yourself things like "Is there anything I can let go of that's holding me back from being kind?" or "How could I be kinder, right now?"

You can work on expanding your sensory acuity. Normally we're quite habitual, and only pay attention to selected sensations connected with our breathing. Try seeing what's just beyond those sensations. And then notice what's just beyond those. Notice not just individual sensations, but how they are connected to each other. Notice subtler sensations of tingling and energy, and how they ebb and flow.

You can work on developing more mindfulness of feelings, especially keeping attention on the heart and solar plexus. Note how different kinds of thoughts make you feel, and how different feelings give rise to various kinds of thinking. Train in recognizing pleasant, unpleasant, and neutral feelings. Train in *accepting* your feelings. Train yourself to recognize suffering as suffering. You can even work on not having goals, and practice simply being with whatever arises, because sometimes we need to work on the skill of not having goals, of being accepting, of letting the mind be at rest. When meditation is nothing but work, it exhausts us and becomes tedious. One of the skills we need to work on in meditation is finding a balance between effort and rest. Settling into that easy state of effortless effort is deeply nourishing.

"I meditate every day. It's just what I do. It's part of who I am. I treat my meditation practice as a craft."

Going Deeper

When the Buddha talked about spiritual practice, he often used analogies drawn from the trades and crafts in the world around him. In the Dhammapada he wrote, "Irrigators channel waters. Fletchers straighten arrows. Carpenters fashion wood. The wise master themselves."[47] At various times he also compared spiritual practitioners to charioteers, cowherds, elephant trainers, gold- and silversmiths, ivory carvers, potters, and even butchers. His followers were all familiar with these occupations, and many would have practiced them. These illustrations gave them a visual and visceral sense of what spiritual practice involves. The mind can be worked with like any other material. And working on the mind is a skill to be developed, like any other. The Buddha even talked about making the mind "pliable" and "workable" as if it were a precious metal.

To work with the mind, we need to understand it; to understand the mind we need to work with it. This is true of all crafts. Many of the Buddha's most important teachings show us how the mind works, particularly in terms of how its movements can either enmesh us in suffering or free us from it. He points to how the mind frees itself from suffering most commonly in terms of the *bojjhangas*, or the seven factors that lead to awakening. These are stages the mind moves through as we work with it. They're descriptions of how spiritually helpful abilities progressively emerge in the mind as we work on it.

1. The first of the seven factors of awakening is *mindfulness*. To work with the mind we need to know what's going on in our experience, so we observe the body, our feelings, and the mind (the first three foundations of mindfulness).[48] We need to know when the hindrances are active, for example, so that we can counteract them.
2. Next is *investigation of mental states* (*dhammavicaya*). We need not just to know what's happening, but to be able to understand it as well. Which of our mental states (and words and actions that flow from them) lead to suffering, and which of them reduce suffering? We learn not just to observe the mind, but to work with it too. Mindfulness and investigation of mental states are like a silversmith testing raw materials, examining their weight and learning what impurities are present so that they can be worked with.

3. Third, we have the *motivation* to practice (*vīriya*). Our being motivated relies on our having faith and confidence in the teachings and practices. We need to be clear about the benefits of practice so we will feel motivated to do it. Motivating ourselves is a major challenge; how we help that motivation to arise and how we remove barriers to it is the theme of this book. Here the silversmith sees that although the raw metal may be impure, it has the potential to be transformed into something beautiful.

4. Next is what I call "*aliveness*"—which is *piti* in Pali. This is a heightened sense of physical and emotional energy that is most often referred to in the context of meditation. Sometimes in meditation the body relaxes and we sense tingling, pleasure, and flows of energy. The pleasant nature of these experiences fascinates the mind and keeps our attention rooted in the body. This awareness of the body's tangible aliveness eventually becomes something we experience not only in meditation, but any time we bring attention to the body. You could imagine this as silver that's had all its impurities removed, so that it's shiny rather than dull.

5. We have *calmness*, or *passaddhi*. The more rooted we are in the present-moment reality of the body and its senses, the less unnecessary thinking and emotional disturbance there is in our meditation. There may still be thinking going on, but it's no longer able to distract us. Instead it just drifts through the mind, like smoke through the sky. Maybe this is like molten silver: calmness is alive and energetic rather than stiff and dead, so it's like quivering liquid metal.

6. As we continue to deepen our meditation practice, we have more experiences of *samādhi*, or *absorption*, which is the sixth factor. We're able to stay with our immediate sensory experience with little or no effort. Our ability to work with the mind is enhanced.

In a state of absorption it becomes easier to cultivate kindness or compassion. In a state of absorption it's also easier for us to observe the impermanence of sensations, feelings, urges, and thoughts as they arise and pass away. We begin to see them as being empty of substance, and are less troubled by them. The effects of meditative absorption and cultivation stay with us outside of meditation as well. If we were to compare this to silversmithing, *samādhi* could be seen as silver being poured from a crucible into a mold; the lip of the crucible focuses the liquid metal in one direction.

7. Finally, because of our heightened ability to observe experiences without the mind being troubled by them, we experience states of imperturbability, or *equanimity*, which is a state of deep, even-minded balance. Here we're at peace. This is the mind made into something pure and beautiful.

These seven states support the arising of enlightenment. I'd like to stress, though, that they are not simply experiences, but are rather skills. Mindfulness is not something we either have or don't have. It's not that it comes into being fully developed. It emerges at first fitfully and incompletely, and in a shallow way. We practice to develop the skill of mindfulness, so that we become aware of ever more aspects of our being, more vividly, and more consistently. The same is true for the other six factors of awakening.

Sometimes we'll have little breakthroughs and experience the body, our feelings, or the mind in new ways. This will be fascinating for a while, and we might be content to rest with our new level of understanding. But we need to keep in mind that this isn't it. Until we reach enlightenment, there are always more skills to be developed.

Reflection

Keep asking yourself, "How can I go a little deeper into this practice?" The next time you're meditating, for example, ask yourself what's just outside of your attention. What are you ignoring? What are you holding on to that you can let go of? In your daily life, keep asking how you can be a little calmer, a little more empathetic, a little kinder. Let these questions draw you deeper into your practice.

Last Words

The possibility of going deeper is always there. The seven factors that lead to awakening (the *bojjhangas*) are skills that emerge as we go deeper, and that also, as we practice them, allow us to go deeper still.

DAY 25

Keep Going Through the Motions

Practice Reminder

Sit for at least five minutes today. Do lots of celebration! Celebrate every time mindfulness reestablishes itself. Celebrate sitting. Celebrate as you record your progress. You can't have too much celebration!

Today

There will be times that you feel like you're just plodding on without any sense of inspiration or reward. Regard this as something to work through. This period of "going through the motions" had a beginning, and it'll have an end too. Believe in yourself. Just keep going and it'll sort itself out.

Strategies

Sometimes you'll find that you're just going through the motions with your meditation practice. You don't have an edge. You've lost touch with the deeper reasons for why you meditate. Maybe you're doing only the bare minimum of meditation. You're not enjoying it. At such times you're going to start wondering if the effort is worthwhile.

In the same teaching where the Buddha talked about incubating our practice like a mother hen sitting on her eggs, he talked about how every time you pick a tool up it looks just like it did the day before. But over the years, even your thumb on the wooden handle will start to wear a groove. Similarly, he points out that when you're meditating, you can't always see that you're making progress, but it's still happening.

Progress isn't always evident. Change can happen gradually, like the wearing away of a piece of wood, like a water pot filling drop by drop, or when we return to the breathing, moment by moment. Sit by sit we wear away unhelpful habits, such as aversion and resistance. We build up new neural pathways in the brain and forge connections between neurons as they fire together. Older pathways, now less used, are dismantled, because the brain likes to conserve resources. All this happens gradually. Maybe you can't see it, but it's happening.

Sometimes we don't notice progress because we adapt to it, day by day, and we see it only when we look back over a period of months or years. Sometimes we realize we've changed only when other people tell us they've seen a difference in us. I've lost count of the number of people who have said that they don't feel any different since they took up meditation, but their spouse says they're much easier to be with. The spouses' comments suggest a significant level of change is taking place, yet apparently from the inside it's not particularly obvious.

Progress doesn't even always *look* like progress. You may experience resistance to meditating because something within you recognizes that a big change is about to happen, and it gets afraid. You experience the resistance and think you're moving backward. But in truth, the opposite is the case; just keep on going, and the breakthrough will happen. This is one reason why meditating through resistance is so powerful.

So, meditate, even if it's a short sit. Meditate, even if you find that you're sleepy. Meditate, even though your mind is all over the place. Meditate, even though it seems that you aren't getting anywhere.

Soften around your resistance, though. It's usually not wise just to power through with a disregard for the more frightened parts of you. They need understanding and reassurance from you. Letting the scared and stuck parts of you know that you care can help them to let go, and you to move on. So persevere, firmly, but also kindly and compassionately.

If nothing else, you're sticking with your intention to sit every day, and in doing so you're developing patience and tenacity. You may be going through the motions, but they're good motions to go through because the journey through them strengthens you. When you hear an inner voice telling you you're not getting anywhere, recognize this as the voice of doubt. Recognize that it's coming from a limited perspective, and probably from a place of fear. Surround those painful feelings of doubt with kindness and empathy, and let faith arise.

There are bound to be times when you're exhausted, you've lost your spark, you're plodding on from day to day and sit to sit, and wondering if you're getting anywhere. And that, believe it or not, is OK. You're human, after all, and humans get tired and sometimes run out of steam. No one can be inspired all the time. If you just keep going, it'll sort itself out. I don't mean to imply that we should push ourselves too hard; there are times we just need to rest. I do mean that we should keep up our meditation practice, however. Sometimes we should let our meditation be the rest we need—not striving, but instead letting go of having goals and allowing the mind to be at ease.

Keep practicing because it's a good thing to do. You'll reconnect with your inspiration. You'll bounce back. You'll remember why you practice. You'll feel alive and enthusiastic again. Lack of inspiration is impermanent.

"I meditate every day. It's just what I do. It's part of who I am. I have the faith to keep going, even when it's difficult."

Going Deeper

Even when our practice is vital and we're energized and engaged, we may sometimes be going through the motions in a different way. The Buddha called the third fetter that holds us back from insight *sīlabbataparāmāsa*. This ungainly compound breaks down into three parts: "being attached to" (*parāmāsa*) "ethical rules" (*sīla*) and "religious practices" (*vata*).

I first met this term translated as "dependence on rites and rituals," which I think is a reflection more of the biases of early translators of the scriptures than it is on the original meaning of the words. Early translators of Buddhist texts, who were often scholars from Protestant backgrounds, looked down on ritual, which they associated with "popish" superstition. They wanted to see Buddhism as a purely rational religion. They assumed that if anything resembling "worship" existed in Buddhism, it must be a corruption of an originally "pure" teaching.

But the third fetter is not about avoiding ritual. Buddhist practice, even from the earliest days, has been full of bowing, chanting, and displays of reverence. The third fetter is about doing the right things for the wrong reasons. Being attached to ethical rules and religious practices means that we are taking tools meant to help us become enlightened, and using them in ways that hold us back from becoming enlightened. For example, when we're discussing the Dharma we may find ourselves trying to impress others with our grasp of the subtleties of the teachings. This is seeking status or praise, which are two of the "eight worldly conditions" that we covered on Day 17. An ego-building concern with status is antithetical to actual Dharma practice, which is meant to help us let go of preoccupations about superiority and inferiority. Knowing a lot about the teachings is not the same thing as mastering them. The point of studying the Buddha's way is to put it into practice. As they say in the Zen tradition, the teachings are a finger pointing at the moon. The point is to look at the moon, not to memorize every crease, wrinkle, and callus on the finger.

In our ethical practice, our aim should be to scrutinize our own actions to notice whether we're causing suffering for ourselves and others, and to notice the extent to which ill will, grasping, and delusion are affecting us. It should be to bring more honesty, kindness, and compassion into our relationship with ourselves and others. Yet it's easy to fall into thinking that the purpose of ethics is to "be good"—to scrupulously follow the rules so we can prove our worth. Even if we no longer believe in a judging God, it seems we can still be stuck trying to prove to him that we're worthy of being rewarded. It's also common that when we first hear about Buddhism's ethical precepts, the first thing we do is think about ways other people fail to observe them. But the precepts exist so we can look at our own behavior, not others'.

Being part of a spiritual tradition can become a source of conceit. We can feel that we're superior to those who follow other faiths, or other teachers, or who don't have a religious practice. We can feel that our own tradition and teacher are the best, and that those things almost automatically make us better than others. Often we seem to think that just by identifying ourselves with something good, we become good. That's not the way personal change happens.

Our meditation practice can be a way of settling for comfortable experiences. It becomes just a pleasant break from life's difficulties, recharging our batteries so that we can find an accommodation with samsara. It becomes a way just to handle stress, or to be more effective in our work, with no true spiritual purpose. When we do this our practice lacks an "edge"—that incisive, investigative quality of *dhammavicaya* that arises when we're clear that the true purpose of meditation is to understand the nature of things, to become enlightened, and to benefit the world.

It's inevitable that we'll get caught up in the fetter of misusing Dharma practices for non-Dharmic ends. We can watch out for this, but we cannot see clearly the extent to which it happens until the fetter of self-view is broken. It's then that we realize how much of our practice did *not* bring us to the realization we've just had—those things that were distractions and dead ends. And it's only then that we can identify those things that were crucial in helping us to wake up to how things really are. In the meantime we need to keep asking ourselves, is my practice helping me to be kinder, more honest, more patient? Am I remembering to directly observe, as best I can, impermanence, unsatisfactoriness, and nonself, rather than just talking about them?

Reflection

Spend a little time reflecting on times that you feel intellectually or morally superior to others. Give some thought to how you might, the next time you're in one of those situations, reconnect with a sense of fallibility and humility, and bear in mind that until we're enlightened we don't really know anything.

Last Words

Keeping the Buddha or some other enlightened being in mind is an excellent way to return the mind to the true purpose of practice. We practice not to be admired or to become a little happier, but to become Buddha.

DAY 26

Find Your Deeper "Why"

Practice Reminder

If you haven't practiced already, let's take care of that now. Reading about meditation isn't of much benefit unless you put it into practice by getting on the cushion. Afterward, celebrate sitting and record your progress.

Today

Are you clear on your life's purpose? Are you clear on why you practice? Let's do an exercise that can help bring those things into focus.

Strategies

The more clearly you see how your meditation practice supports your deeper purpose and values in life, the easier it is to remain committed to it. But first we have to recognize that purpose.

Our purpose—something we all have, even if we don't realize it—is not imposed from outside, but is something we find for ourselves in order to give life meaning. It manifests as a deep inner longing that shapes important life choices, even if we're usually not at all clear where it's taking us. Given the nature of modern life, that's understandable. We don't have time to reflect, and few people encourage us to do so anyway. So we just keep on plugging away, day after day, trying to keep on top of work, family responsibilities, and keeping ourselves fed and housed. You have a meditation practice, which is an expression of your purpose, so you probably have a clearer idea than most people of what it is. You're already halfway there.

I'd like to suggest three exercises that can help you connect with your life's deeper meaning. To do the first of these exercises, make sure you have at least ten minutes available when you can be in a relaxed and unhurried frame of mind. You will also need something to write with.

Exercise 1: Hear What's Important to You

Imagine it's ten, fifteen, or perhaps twenty years from now.[49] You walk into a large hall and find it's full of people. What a surprise! It seems like almost everyone you know is here: colleagues going back decades, friends, family, neighbors, people you know from volunteer projects, fellow spiritual practitioners. What's going on? It turns out that they're all there to celebrate you! One by one they stand up and talk. They share what they admire about you, what they've learned from you, and what contributions you've made to their lives and to the world. Listen to what these people say. Then having heard them, write down the points that really stood out for you.

This is what I heard one time that I did this exercise. For the sake of explaining this process I've kept my list to a brief summary of just three things:

1. People appreciated my kindness.
2. People were grateful to me for having helped them find greater peace in their lives.
3. My partner appreciated the love, empathy, and support I'd shown her over the years.

If you feel blocked while doing this exercise and nothing seems to come up, you're not doing it wrong. It's probably just that the conditions aren't right. Try coming back to it when you feel more at ease. Perhaps try it after you've meditated, or while you're lying in bed.

What happened in this exercise is that you tricked yourself into seeing your core values. These are the things that are most important to you. These are the things you value. They represent your deeper purpose, which you may not even been clear you had until you heard your inner wisdom speak though the voices of other people.

Now how can we connect those values with our meditation practice?

Exercise 2: Create Value Statements

Find some time when you can be at ease and reflect. Take each of the things you wrote down in the first exercise and think about why it is important to you. How does it make life meaningful? What does it contribute to your life?

Take as long as you need for this exercise. You can start your value statements with things like "It's important to me . . ." or "I value . . ." for example. There are no wrong answers. Bear in mind that I've kept mine very concise because I simply want to illustrate the general principle of how we create value statements. Yours might be much more detailed.

Having clarified our values, we now need to see how our meditation practice can be—or is already—aligned with them.

Exercise 3: Connect Your Practice with Your Values

Take each of the value statements above and express how meditating helps you live your life's purpose. These sentences can start with something like "I meditate every day because . . ."

Here's what came up for me during these reflections. This is just a brief summary, and you might want to go into much more depth.

What I heard	The value this expresses	How daily meditation supports and expresses that value.
People appreciated my kindness.	It's important to me to relate to people with kindness and empathy. Connecting in this way brings me a sense of peace.	I meditate every day because it makes me a kinder person.
People were grateful to me for having helped them find greater peace in their lives.	My life feels meaningful when I'm making a positive impact on the world. Working with others helps me to change as well as them.	Meditating daily gives me the calmness, clarity, and depth of practice I need so that I can help others.
My spouse appreciated the love, empathy, and support I'd shown her over the years.	Loving and being loved nourishes me deeply. It gives me joy, emotional sustenance, and energy.	I meditate daily so that I can stay intimately and vulnerably connected with my own heart and my partner's.

Now I have greater clarity about the purpose of meditating daily. I meditate every day not because I'm "supposed" to meditate, or because meditating every day makes me a "good Buddhist," or because it makes me a bit happier. My practice exists to make me a kinder person, to give my life meaning, and to sustain and deepen the intimate connections I have with those I love. Ideally, my practice expresses and supports my values.

Clarifying the role of meditation in my life can also clarify what I do in my practice and how I do it. Having become clearer, for example, that I aspire to be kinder, I can aim to sit kindly, regard myself kindly, treat myself kindly, and to consider others with as much kindness and compassion as possible. I can notice habits that are unkind, and seek to change them. So these reflective practices can help us refine our practice.

Becoming clearer about your life's purpose changes how you understand your practice. You're not just meditating to find a little calmness, but because it's contributing in various ways to deeply meaningful aims you have in life. You're seeing your practice as a vitally significant part of your life. Why, then, would you ever want to neglect it?

"I meditate every day. It's just what I do. It's part of who I am. My practice helps me express my life's deepest values."

Going Deeper

The Buddha said there were five things that everyone should frequently call to mind:[50]

1. I am subject to old age; I am not exempt from old age.
2. I am subject to sickness; I am not exempt from sickness.
3. I am subject to death; I am not exempt from death.
4. I must be parted and separated from everything I hold dear and beloved.
5. I am the owner of my actions and heir to my actions. My actions give birth to me, accompany me, and shelter me. I shall be the heir of whatever actions I do, whether beneficial or harmful.

You might think it would be a bit of a downer to keep reminding yourself of death, illness, and loss, but doing so can be surprisingly life-affirming. When married couples have been asked to reflect on the fact that death will eventually separate them, they feel more loving and appreciative of each other, and things about each other that used to bother them no longer matter as much. Similarly, when parents remember that each phase their child goes through—baby, toddler, preschooler, and so on—is fleeting, they cherish each of these stages of life more fully, rather than focusing on the more difficult parts of being a parent.

In a way the first four reflections—on old age, sickness, death, and loss—can be summarized as, "You don't have much time here." The final reflection—on our actions—asks, "How do you plan to make use of that time?" Remembering that we have a limited amount of time on earth helps us to become more intentional about our lives. We're more likely, then, to live our values.

You might have noticed the simplicity and straightforwardness of the first four reflections. They're stated so clearly that a child could understand them. The fifth, on the other hand, is strangely complex and multifaceted, and is in desperate need of being unpacked.

The topic of the fifth reflection is action. This is *kamma* in Pali, which is more familiar to us in its Sanskrit form, *karma*. While karma is popularly thought of as some kind of cosmic rewards-and-punishment system—the "invisible hand" of the moral marketplace—karma simply means "action." Karma is about how we choose our actions, and how those choices shape the kind of experience we have. But it's not about any old choices, like whether you prefer coffee or tea, or gardening to watching TV. Karmic actions are those that are ethically significant. Essentially, karma is any action we take that reinforces, through repetition, either our skillful or our unskillful traits. It's what shapes our character, for good or bad.

To unpack the fifth reflection:

> We *own* our actions, in that only we can take responsibility for them. No one else can do this for us.
>
> We are the *heirs* to our actions because we live with their consequences.
>
> Our actions give birth to us. (The Pali says they are the "womb" from which we come.) In other words, who we are now grows from the ethical habits we have cultivated in the past.
>
> Our actions accompany us on our lives. (The Pali says they are our *family*. This means that that they are so close to us they are in a way a part of us, and like relatives they can either help or harm us.)

Our actions are our *shelter* because the character we create through them may or may not give us the resilience to weather whatever life may send our way.

The more we develop qualities of compassion, patience, wise perspectives, perseverance, resilience, and so on, the stronger the shelter we build for ourselves, and the more we can live life with calm and dignity, even when circumstances are hard. I'm not talking about rugged individualism, which is how "character" is often understood. Taking responsibility for ourselves can mean that our actions and decisions lead to us connecting more with others, building loving networks of support and compassion, so that we shelter others and they shelter us. The roots of trees in the forest interlink deep in the earth, so that the force of a strong wind pushing against one tree is absorbed by its neighbors. We can take responsibility for our own lives, but that doesn't mean we have to be alone in them.

Reflecting on these five remembrances is itself a powerful karmic activity. It changes our perspective on life, changes what we value, shapes who we are, and in doing so it shapes the way we experience life. The more we reflect wisely on these five insights, the less suffering we'll experience as we encounter life's obstacles, which include old age, sickness, death, and loss. The more we reflect on these, the more prepared we are when they affect our lives.

The Buddha suggested that we're intoxicated by youth, health, life, and by the hope of holding on to the things we cherish. Our drunken heedlessness makes us imagine, especially when we're young, that life and health are an inexhaustible resource, and so we don't value how fleeting they are. We imagine we're immune to aging, sickness, and death. When we're young and healthy we tend to see those who are old and sick as being almost a different species from us. We find it hard to accept the reality that we and they are simply at different stages on the same path, and that old age and sickness are steadily getting closer. It can be a shock when reality clashes with our delusions. The Buddha's reflections soften that shock.

We overcome this intoxication and sober up to the reality of our mortal nature by reflecting repeatedly that there is no line dividing us from the elderly, the infirm, and the dead. We exist on a continuum in which those things are creeping up on us (or we on them), moment by moment. Realizing this, we can see that whatever has been dear to us—whatever we value—is either in line with our deeper values (such as loving connections with friends and family) or irrelevant to them (such as spending more time in the office to impress our boss). We are responsible for how we live our lives, so it's up to us what we do. Our actions can either create happiness for ourselves and others, or they can create suffering. It's up to us.

Reflection

At a time when you can sit undisturbed, allow your mind to be still and your heart to be open. Then, spend some time turning the five reflections over in your mind. Feel each one in your heart. See what implications each evokes. Write those down as statements that can guide the way you live.

Last Words

We are not here for long. What's the best way for you to use the time that's given to you?

DAY 27

To Defeat Māra, Congratulate Him

Practice Reminder

You meditate every day. It's just what you do. It's part of who you are. Sit. Celebrate. Record your progress. Every damn day!

Today

Try seeing anything that threatens to derail your practice as being Māra—a personification of spiritual bewilderment. Recognizing Māra and (crucially) congratulating him on the cleverness of his tricks is a powerful practice for regaining our mental freedom.

Strategies

The inner voice that dissuades us from meditating every day is the same one that hinders our progress toward enlightenment in other ways. It's the same voice that leads us into anger, fearfulness, conceit, and addictive behaviors. It's the same one that suggests that enlightenment isn't for us. The Buddhist tradition has a name for that voice: Māra. This word is a personal name that comes from the same ancient Indo-European root as the words *mortality* and *murder*. Māra is the name given to the part of us that wants to "kill" our spiritual practice.

In the early scriptures, meditators often see Māra in human form: often one with a fine appearance. But he can also appear as an animal or demon, or manifest as a frightening sound or an earthquake—whatever helps him turn the mind from practice. Nowadays when we meet Māra it's usually in the form of thoughts, feelings, and impulses. Because he speaks to us with our own voice, he can be very convincing. This voice often comes across as being compassionately concerned for our well-being. He says, "I'm exhausted! I really deserve a day off from meditating," and we think it's us that's talking. He can appear as anxiety or depression. He might just be a distracting urge that causes us to miss our daily meditation without even realizing it.

The strategies in this book are an armory of tools for defeating Māra. Before we learned to use those tools, there were always days when Māra could defeat us by convincing us not to meditate. Now, we know how to defeat him. In the process of establishing and maintaining a regular meditation practice we've made it harder for Māra to take over our minds, because we've gotten better at staying on track through not believing everything we think, not being manipulated by our feelings, through surfing our urges, and so on.

Māra may have less power over us now, but he is still there, and will be there even once we're enlightened. The Buddha himself met Māra often, showing that conquering Māra is not the same thing as getting rid of him entirely. Māra still followed the Buddha around and made attempts to influence him, although he was never successful in doing so. Hopefully at this point Māra is no longer be able to prevent you from practicing daily. Maybe occasionally he can pull a fast one and cause you to miss a day, but you know now that missing a day ocassionally does not mean you're not a Rock-Solid Daily Meditator. You slip, you fall, you get straight back up again. If that's not happening for you yet, keep applying these strategies. You'll get there.

But Māra can still defeat us in other ways. Any time we act unskillfully, that's Māra at work. He still has the power to convince us that we *must* get angry, or anxious, or despairing, or that there is some perfect object of craving that will take away our dissatisfactions if we can only get hold of it. He still makes us suffer, and will do until we're enlightened. Only then will our unskillful tendencies, and the suffering they cause, be abandoned. Until then, we still have work to do in weakening Māra.

The most important thing to recognize is that we can't defeat Māra by arguing with him. He's the voice of resistance that I described earlier as the captain of our inner debate team. He's spent his entire existence learning our weaknesses and how to manipulate them. And hatred *is* Māra, so if we try to get rid of him by hating him we're just giving him a bit of exercise—and a good laugh at our expense. Our approach needs to be subtle and smart. There are two parts to it: first, we recognize Māra, and second, we congratulate him.

In the early scriptures, every single time a spiritual practitioner recognizes the trickster and says, "I see you, Māra," Māra disappears. Once we recognize him, he loses his power over us. Recognizing Māra is one of the most powerful practices I've ever done. I've sometimes woken in the middle of the night, intensely anxious about something. Then I remember: *This is Māra! He's tricking me into suffering!* When I recognize this, I immediately gain a degree of freedom that wasn't there before. The anxious feelings and thoughts are still there, but they no longer control me, and I'm more at peace.

Yet there is an even deeper practice. Instead of just recognizing Māra, I congratulate him. I heartily commend him for how well he's been able to fool me. I give him a mental handclap. I express my admiration of how the anxiety he's created has hoodwinked me into thinking that I *have* to suffer. I praise him for the way that the catastrophizing thoughts I'd been having seemed *real*, rather than just things I'd imagined. And so I'll say, "Wow, Māra! You really had me going there. That was such a clever illusion. What amazing special effects! Really convincing! Brilliant!"

When I do this, my suffering vanishes. Often the sensations that I'd experienced as anxiety are still there, but I no longer perceive them as anxiety. Instead, they're a beautiful tingling aliveness that fills me with energy. Looking for my suffering, I can no longer find it. I'm at peace, but also full of joy.

You can recognize and congratulate Māra whenever any state that causes suffering hijacks your mind: despondency, anger, hatred, resentment, craving, resistance, and so on. Any time you are suffering or in a reactive state, Māra has taken control of your mind. Recognizing Māra's trickery and congratulating him on how cleverly he's fooled you allows you to reclaim your mind and dispel suffering.

Sometimes, even when I'm not particularly suffering, I watch the mind, observing Māra's thoughts, feelings, and impulses come into being. As they appear, I recognize them and give Māra some hearty applause. A little impatience comes up, and I see and applaud Māra. A critical thought appears, and I not only see Mara but also heartily congratulate him. I recommend trying this in meditation and in daily life. He's nothing if not persistent, and he'll give you plenty to observe. On a good day you can rest in freedom, taking down Māra's phantom projections as if you were shooting Space Invaders on a 1980s arcade game.

This is the most powerful strategy I know. It's possible that what I've described might not make much sense to you unless you've practiced other things I've discussed, like knowing suffering as suffering, being able to accept painful feelings, observing impermanence, and looking at the finely detailed texture (and emptiness) of feelings. For me, those practices were precursors that made it possible for me to relate to Māra in the way I've described. And yet I've introduced this approach to many people who have also found it helpful. The most difficult thing about it is, as always, remembering to do it.

Establishing a Rock-Solid Daily Meditation Practice represents a major victory over Māra. He really doesn't want you to meditate. He represents deep habits of craving and aversion that your meditation practice is going to destroy. When he stops you from meditating he's engaged in a battle for survival. When, day after day after day, you defeat his schemes, you show him who's the boss. Dealing with unskillful thoughts and habits is a challenge, but as you engage with them you can know that Māra is on the defensive, and is destined to lose.

Once we win the struggle with Māra, we're finally free—awake, enlightened. And at that point our minds are filled with unshakable confidence and compassion for all that lives. There is, so they say, no longer the slightest trace of selfishness or ill will, and none can be stirred up. Māra may still walk with us and talk to us, as he did with the Buddha. But, as with the Buddha, he can never control us. Our minds are free, and with that freedom comes peace.

So keep going—with the support of a Rock-Solid Daily Meditation Practice—until freedom becomes your home.

"I meditate every day. It's just what I do. It's part of who I am. It frees my mind from the bonds of Māra. It is my path to full awakening."

Going Deeper

In Buddhism, ethics is not about being good. Although the Buddha did use terms like *good* and *bad*, this was usually when he taught in verse, when simple terms are often needed, or when he was speaking to uneducated people, who needed, straightforward messages to remember.

When he was having more technical discussions with serious practitioners he more often used the terms *skillful* (*kusala*) and *unskillful* (*akusala*). These are terms I've used throughout the book, although so far I haven't defined them. Maybe you were already familiar with them in this context, or perhaps you just thought that they were a peculiar quirk of my writing. Either way, I think there's value in poking around under the hood to see what the function of these words is.

So let's think about what skill is. What does it mean to do something in a skilled way?

If you have skill, you're able to achieve something that you set out to do. Say a skilled potter wants to make a particular kind of pot: because they've practiced a lot, they know what they're doing, and they understand their tools and their materials, and so they're able to make that kind of pot. They have the skill to accomplish what they set out to do. A person who lacks skill cannot do that. Being able to achieve your aims is what it means to be skilled or unskilled.

The Buddha used *skillful* and *unskillful* as ethical and meditative terms. So, what are we trying to create through our actions and our meditation practice? The point of practice is to liberate ourselves from suffering. It's to become happier, more contented, more fulfilled, and to have more of a sense of meaning in our lives. It's to have a better life and, out of compassion, to help other people have that experience as well. These are the things in which we're developing skill.

In Buddhism, skillfulness is all about what creates freedom from suffering. It's not about "being good." The Buddha didn't tell us to abandon greed, hatred, and delusion because they are bad, but because they cause suffering. In fact, he said that if they didn't cause suffering, he wouldn't tell us to abandon them:

> *If giving up the unskillful led to harm and suffering, I would not say: "Give up the unskillful." But giving up the unskillful leads to welfare and happiness, so I say: "Give up the unskillful."*[51]

This is mind-blowing when you think about it. The founder of one of the world's major religions said that it would be fine to be deluded, greedy, and hateful if those things made us happy. But they don't.

The thoughts, words, and actions that free us from suffering are skillful. Those that do the opposite are unskillful. Skillful qualities—those that help us move closer to freedom from suffering—include confidence, trust, patience, courage, kindness, empathy, compassion, appreciation, humility, and so on. We're acting unskillfully when we're in the grip of unskillful states of mind that create suffering. So this is what I think the Buddha may have had in mind when he was using the terms *skillful* and *unskillful*, which might seem strange at first glance. It's all about what works.

It's an interesting shift of perspective to think about ethics in terms of skill. It's different from how we might have been raised to see things. We may have been raised to see things in terms of good and bad. We get caught up in the idea of people themselves being good and bad. But it's only *actions* that can be skillful or unskillful. You can't talk about an unskillful person because no person is entirely skillful or unskillful.

Lots of people think of themselves as being good or bad. They want to see themselves and be seen by others as being good. This is often a disastrous move, because when we want to see ourselves as good we inevitably end up in denial about our unskillful tendencies. When we want others to see us as good we become dishonest. Lots of people do the opposite and become convinced that they are inherently bad, or unworthy, and because of this they're miserable—as well as sadly mistaken. You may be one of those people. Whether you are or not, you probably know some of them, and your impression of them in most cases is probably that they are lovely people with many fine qualities. They're probably kind and thoughtful, and you probably benefit from being with them. And that's how other people likely see you if you think you're a bad person.

We're all a mixture of skillful and unskillful qualities. No one is all one or all the other. And spiritual training—or at least a lot of spiritual training—is about, on the one hand, exercising and strengthening the skillful, and on the other hand recognizing and letting go of the unskillful. Except that we do not own these qualities. There is no self there to cultivate the skillful or let go of the unskillful. It is skillful qualities of wisdom and mindfulness that recognize the benefits of encouraging other skillful qualities, and that see that for the benefit of whatever-it-is-we-are, unskillful qualities need to be let go of. *We* do not practice; our skillfulness does. As practice deepens, we have a progressively stronger sense of "allowing" and of "letting happen." Skillful qualities simply emerge, often surprising us. Practice is not something we do. It's something that happens.

In a way, skillful qualities are more fundamental to our being than the unskillful ones. One image in the scriptures sees the doubt-filled mind as like a jar full of water into which mud has been stirred. Shaken up, the water is a mess. You can't drink it. You can't see through it. You can't see your reflection in it. All we have to do, though, is wait. Just let the jar be still. The swirl of the water slows down and stops. The mud begins to settle out. Eventually the water becomes clear and pure. All we have to do is let it sit. If you think about it, the water was never really contaminated. The water molecules were not fundamentally changed by the presence of the mud. In its essence the water was always pure. The mud settling out just allowed water's true nature to reveal itself.

And this is what we do in meditation, too. As we sit, we catch unruly thoughts agitating the jar of the mind. We can't see deeply into ourselves. We can't reflect. But if we keep allowing the mind to come back to rest, those swirling thoughts settle down. The mind becomes clear. The skillfulness of the mind is revealed, and it's kinder, happier. As skillful qualities become more evident, they reach a tipping point and self-organize to reveal greater degrees of wisdom and compassion.

Some teachings say that these are the inherent qualities of the mind, and the mind has never been truly contaminated. In its essence it has always been pure. Stillness allows us to see this. We establish a Rock-Solid Daily Meditation Practice—we commit to sit—so that this can happen.

Reflection

In your next sit, let your eyes be soft—relaxed and almost unfocused—and let your field of attention be expansive and open. Notice how the mind, as it settles, becomes clearer and kinder. Notice those times when there is a reduced sense of "doing" and a heightened sense of a natural unfolding within you—a process that isn't under conscious control, but that simply happens as skillful qualities collaborate and support each others' arising.

Last Words

There are times we feel like we're doing something in meditation. But the longer we practice, the more we can have a sense that practice is something that is just happening. Our practice is doing itself.

DAY 28

Keep Going to the Tipping Point

Practice Reminder

Your self-doubts and self-criticisms are just Māra trying to derail your practice. Recognize him, congratulate him on how clever he is, and then sit. It's just what you do. Keep sitting, daily. Celebrate every time. And you might, beyond this course, want to keep tracking your sits. I do (at least some of the time), and I find it helpful and encouraging.

Today

As we collect and implement more and more strategies, intelligently adapting them to help us achieve the aim of daily practice, we get to the point where it's easier to sit every day than it is to miss a day. If you're not at that point yet, you will be one day. (Just remember the intelligently adapting part!)

Strategies

Three weeks into leading a Get Your Sit Together course, I asked the participants how many of them felt better about themselves now that they were meditating regularly. Every hand went up. Having succeeded where they'd failed so many times before, they felt more confident and had shed the negative self-image that had attached itself to their meditation practice.

As you've developed the daily meditation habit, you may have noticed other habits starting to change, sometimes spontaneously and in unexpected ways. People find that they naturally want to eat more healthily. They're less drawn to social media. An urge to start exercising may appear from nowhere. They feel effortlessly inspired to start practicing a musical instrument they've neglected for years. This relates to the concept of meditation as a keystone habit, as I discussed in the introduction. When you feel good about yourself, which happens when you've overcome long-standing doubts about your ability to meditate regularly—you're more likely to do things that keep you feeling good. When you're meditating regularly your mind is clearer and your emotions more settled, and so you make better decisions. This is a classic positive feedback loop, where good things happening help other good things to happen.

As the understanding that you are the kind of person who meditates every day becomes more strongly internalized, meditating every day becomes effortless. It just happens. Hopefully this is happening for you now, and you've developed a settled, self-sustaining habit of daily meditation that doesn't rely on willpower. You just want to do it, and you know how to handle any resistance should it arise. It's easier to meditate than it is not to meditate.

This can all flow so effortlessly that you may feel as if something creative is expressing itself through you. You're becoming a channel for wiser and kinder aspects of yourself that have been there all along, but haven't had a way to express themselves fully. You've certainly heard from them before, but not enough that they've directed the flow of your life. But now you've opened a channel of communication through which your inner wisdom can express itself. As this continues, it may not be long before you've reached a tipping point where a day without meditating becomes unthinkable.

"I meditate every day. It's just what I do. It's part of who I am. I meditate because it's what I want to do."

Going Deeper

"Entering the stream" is a common and important expression in the early Buddhist texts. It's one I've mentioned several times. The significance of stream entry is that it's the first *irreversible* insight we have into the nature of reality. It's the beginning of a process of enlightenment that is guaranteed to continue until we reach the same degree of awakening that the Buddha himself had.

Stream entry is a tipping point, marking the arising of transcendental insight—that is, an insight that breaks the fetters keeping us from enlightenment. Although this tipping point isn't easy to reach, it's doable. Many people have become stream entrants. You don't have to be a monk or nun who devotes dozens of hours to meditation every week. Even people who are holding down demanding jobs and raising kids can reach the point of stream entry. It's more to do with the consistency and quality of your practice than it is about the quantity of meditation you do.

The supports and criteria for becoming a stream entrant are laid out in the scriptures. Along the way I've been describing many of the steps involved. Stream entry has four supports:[52]

1. Associating with people of integrity (ideally other Dharma practitioners, but any ethical, wise friends and role models will help)
2. Listening to the true teaching (choose your teachers carefully)
3. Intelligently applying your mind (which is the theme of this book)

4. Practicing the teachings in line with the teachings (not using Dharma practice to build your ego, for example)

Developing a Rock-Solid Daily Meditation Practice is an invaluable catalyst for spiritual progress, not just because of the benefits that come from meditating regularly, but because in order to establish a regular practice you have to come to understand yourself more clearly, learn what helps or hinders your meditation, apply yourself intelligently to the task, and learn from the feedback—in the form of your practice happening or not happening—that your life delivers to you.

What the four supporting factors lead to is the breaking of the three fetters. (These are the first three out of ten that are broken on the way to full awakening.) These three fetters, which we've dealt with individually, are as follows:

1. Self-view
2. Doubt
3. Attachment to ethical rules and religious practices as ends in themselves

Usually we come to the Dharma because we want to be better people. We want to get better at handling stress and to be happier in our lives. We want to inflict less suffering on others. The Dharma, with its promise of self-improvement, is just what we need. It can be so exciting to discover it! Well, the self-improvement part is great, but the whole enlightenment thing? That might seem a bit pie in the sky. Who has that amount of commitment? And frankly it doesn't sound too attractive. What's wrong with a bit of attachment? Life would be so dull without it.

Right there we can see the three fetters. We have a view of ourselves where we think we're maybe capable of *some* change, but that we're fundamentally broken and stuck. This is doubt: *How could I—poor, stuck, broken me—ever become enlightened? I'll leave that to other people.*

Those doubts seem to be confirmed as we discover it's harder to change than we'd imagined. Habits are stubborn things. Even after years of meditation we find that we're making the same mistakes, and still hurting ourselves and others in the same old ways. This feeds back into our self-view, convincing us that there must indeed be something unchangeable and broken about us. We believe that we need to hide this brokenness from others, since if they knew what we were really like, they'd dislike us. This kind of belief is very common.

Believing we're broken, we look for validation outside of ourselves. All the beautiful and elegant practices the Dharma offers us for seeing through the illusion of self and awakening to reality become props for supporting our ego. We seek happiness within the worldly *dhammas*. We want to think of ourselves as good people because we practice. We want other people to see us as good because of our deep understanding of the teachings, or because we are part of the "best" spiritual community, following the most wonderful teacher. Hiding our brokenness from others, we don't deeply share our struggles with our companions in the spiritual life, and so we don't learn from our mistakes and move on from them. Hiding behind a façade, we're almost frozen in place, barely progressing. All the things we're doing might look good on the surface, but we're doing many of them for the wrong reasons—with ego-building motives.

But . . . *if* we keep associating with wise friends and role-models; *if* we're receptive to the Dharma; *if* we stay curious and keep applying our minds intelligently to the teachings and to our lives; *if* we keep practicing sincerely—then the Dharma will work its magic on us.

Dharma practice encourages us to observe impermanence, and to recognize that everything that constitutes us is changing all the time. If we keep reflecting on such things and observing change, then at some point—and this may take many years—we are sure to realize, "Where, in all this incessant change, could there ever have been a permanent, unchanging self?"

If the conditions are right, we recognize that the kind of self we once thought ourselves to have does not and never has existed. There is no fixed self. Our imagined irredeemable brokenness is not even a burden that we set down. The only burden was that we thought it existed in the first place. Seeing this is tremendously liberating and joyful.

The first fetter—self-view—has broken.

We now see ourselves in a completely new way: the path to awakening exists and we know we are on it. The insight of breaking through the illusion of self is a permanent one, and so we'll never again doubt our ability to go all the way. Or if we do, the doubt is fleeting, and easily dispelled by reminding ourselves of Dharma teachings, or even by looking again to see if we have a self and realizing with laughter that it's not there.

The second fetter—doubt—has broken.

We realize with amazement that the evidence is everywhere that there is no self. We see thoughts arising without a thinker, bodily movements happening without a mover. How could we have not seen this before! It was right there, all along! We just didn't let ourselves see it.

We realize that a lot of our "practice" had been done with faulty motives. We'd been busy trying to be "good," hoping that the approval of others would fix our imagined brokenness. We'd been busy reading and talking about impermanence rather than seeing impermanence directly. We'd continued imagining a self and thinking it was something we had to get rid of, rather than realizing we can't get rid of something that never existed. But now we can see the difference between practice as the path we are on toward enlightenment, and practice as an expression of the *loka-dhammas*—the motions we go through to compensate for our imagined brokennesss.

The third fetter—attachment to ethical rules and religious practices—has broken.

These three fetters break almost simultaneously, in one movement, like dominos falling. And so we enter the stream that carries us the rest of the way. I call stream-entry "entry-level awakening," because there's a long way still to go, but the process has begun. A tipping point has been reached, and full enlightenment is assured. We're in the stream, being carried along. And practice comes so easily that we couldn't not do it if we tried.

"I meditate every day. It's just what happens. It's part of the mystery that I am. And it carries me along the stream toward full awakening."

Reflection

Today's reflection is not about today's reading specifically. Instead it's about the journey we've been on together. How has it been for you, I wonder? I know it's a hard thing to develop the habit of becoming a Rock-Solid Daily Meditator. You'll have had ups and downs. Perhaps moments of joy and despair. Perhaps this is a good time to think about what's worked well for you and what's worked less well. Maybe you could make a list of each, and some notes about what you might do differently. Cast an eye back over the book and see what tools you might have overlooked, or put down somewhere and forgotten about. In the journey that is the rest of your life—and may it be a long and fulfilling one—you may want to revisit them. We can never have too many tools.

Last Words

There is a point in our spiritual journey where there is so much momentum in your practice that it carries you relentlessly on. This is not a scary experience. It's a joyful feeling that there are no real obstacles to progress. Observing the impermanence of everything that constitutes "you" is the key to reaching this tipping point.

AFTERWORD

The Rest of Your Life

By now, with all these strategies at your disposal, I hope you're either meditating daily or making good progress in that direction. Here are a few points to bear in mind regarding your meditation habit:

- Remember, habits are not built overnight. It can take months for them to consolidate, and even then, they require reflection and further action to maintain. Please keep returning to this book, brushing up on the skills and strategies it teaches.
- Keep repeating the mantra: You meditate every day. It's just what you do. It's part of who you are. *You don't miss days.*
- Meditate, even if it's just for five minutes, sometime between waking in the morning and going back to sleep at night.
- For as long as you find it useful, keep tracking your sits by putting a check mark in your calendar, or by some other means. It's inspiring to have an unbroken streak of "on" days, and you'll get to the point when you really don't want to break the chain.
- Watch out for the complacency I described being tripped up by in Day 21. Often, we'll have success at doing something and forget that it was the diligent application of certain skills that got us there. We start to think that the habit simply happens, and so we forget that we need strategies to create it and hold it in place.
- Keep celebrating! Feel good about having kept true to your intentions, and about the very fact of meditating.
- Keep your values and life goals in mind, and see your meditation practice as a way to fulfill them.

- Keep recognizing Māra, in all his many forms, and congratulate him when he's caught you out. He won't like being found out, but he enjoys being admired, and it's better to send him off pleased with himself. With any luck it'll keep him distracted for a while.

Above all, know that you have the power to overcome any obstacle that stands in your way. You can do this. You already are doing it. After all, you meditate every day. It's just what you do. It's part of who you are.

APPENDIX 1

Before and After Sitting

Some people find it helpful to recite verses immediately before meditation. In Buddhist practice we might recite the refuges and precepts. The refuges orient us toward awakening by calling to mind the Buddha, as an example of an enlightened practitioner and teacher; the Dharma, as the path and practices that help us to become enlightened like the Buddha was; and the Sangha, as the spiritual community that teaches, inspires, and supports us along the way. (Even this book is an experience of sangha; you have not been alone while reading it.)

Before Sitting

Below, I've presented the refuges and precepts in English. Even after having chanted these in Pali for over forty years, and despite having studied Pali at university, I still find chanting them in English more heartfelt and moving. I've rendered the precepts both in terms of what we abstain from, and what we cultivate. We can recite these words mindfully, taking in their meaning, as a kind of meditation before the meditation.

The Three Refuges

To the Buddha for refuge I go.
To the Dharma for refuge I go.
To the Sangha for refuge I go.
(Recite three times).

The Five Precepts

1. I undertake to abstain from harming living beings, and vow to live with compassion.
2. I undertake to abstain from taking what's not given, and vow to live with generosity.
3. I undertake to abstain from sexual misconduct, and vow to live with respect for others.
4. I undertake to abstain from untruth, and vow to live with honesty and integrity.
5. I undertake to abstain from intoxication, and vow to live mindfully.

After Sitting

After meditation it can be meaningful to dedicate the fruits of our practice to all beings. The "Dedication of Merit" below is adapted from an eighth-century text by Shantideva, *The Guide to the Bodhisattva's Way of Life*.[53]

Reciting these verses, we remind ourselves once again of the larger context and meaning of what we're doing.

Dedication of Merit

May the skillful qualities arising
From this period of practice
Help alleviate the suffering of all beings.

My entire being throughout my existences,
My possessions,

And my skillful qualities of body, speech, and mind
I make available, withholding nothing,
For the benefit of all beings.

Just as the earth and other elements
Are serviceable in many ways
To the infinite number of beings
Inhabiting limitless space;
So may I become
That which maintains all beings
Situated throughout space,
So long as all have not attained to peace.

Shanti! Shanti! Shanti![54]

APPENDIX 2

Meditation Instructions

Complete beginners to meditation might find it helpful to read over the instructions below, although it might be more effective to listen to some of the guided meditations accompanying this book. It's possible that some established meditators will also find something helpful here.

Simple Mindfulness of Breathing

- Set a timer with a gentle sound. If you're a complete beginner to meditation, five minutes is fine.
- It's better to sit upright than to lie down, because lying down can make us sleepy. But if you are genuinely unable to sit upright, feel free to lie. Whichever you do, make sure your spine is straight so that you can breathe freely.
- Take a few slow, deep breaths, just to help you to arrive in the body, and let the eyes gently close.
- Let your eyes be at rest behind your eyelids, with the muscles around them relaxed, and let the focus within your eyes be soft.
- Notice how the softness of the eyes allows your inner field of attention to be soft, open, and receptive, too, so that you can effortlessly be aware of sensations of the breathing arising from all over the body.
- Notice how soft waves of movement and sensation sweep through the entire body with every in breath and out breath.

- Let yourself notice the richness of this experience, and how every sensation is connected to every other.
- Let your attention rest gently on the soft waves of the breathing as they sweep through the body.
- You might find that you're able to stay with this experience while thoughts arise and pass away in the background. That's fine. Just let those thoughts come and go.
- Sometimes, though, you might find that your thoughts take you away from the sensations of the breathing. That's normal. Just let go of the story you've been drawn into, let the eyes soften again, and return to noticing the waves of the breathing.
- Be grateful every time your mind returns to mindful awareness.
- When your gentle alarm sounds, take your time. When it feels right to do so, begin to move the body slowly and allow your eyes to gently open, bringing your mindful attention more fully into the world again.

Simple Loving-kindness Meditation

- As with the previous meditation, set a gentle timer, and sit or lie in a comfortable, open way that allows you to have a straight spine so that you can breathe freely.
- Let your closed eyes be soft, so that your inner field of attention softens and becomes receptive and open.
- While still gently aware of the eyes, recall what it's like to look with love. You might want to recall a specific experience of looking at a child, a lover, a friend, or a pet.

- Notice how qualities such as warmth, gentleness, and appreciation arise in and around the eyes.
- And now notice that those qualities pervade your attention as you become more fully aware of your body, your heart, your thoughts, and anything that arises within you. With kind eyes, meet everything with warmth.
- Offer yourself support and encouragement by saying, over and over again, "May you be at ease. May you be happy. May you be kind to yourself and others."
- Take your time saying these phrases, leaving pauses between each one. During these pauses, simply be aware of your own being, with kindness.
- After a while, call to mind someone you know. It could be a friend, someone you struggle to get along with, or a relative stranger.
- Recall that this person, just like you, feels happiness and unhappiness, and that those feelings are just as real and vivid to them as yours are to you.
- Offer them support, encouragement, and warmth by saying, over and over again, "May you be at ease. May you be happy. May you be kind to yourself and others."
- Again, take your time. In the pauses between the phrases, continue to notice yourself and the other person in a warm, supportive way.
- When your alarm sounds, sit for a moment, making no effort, but simply resting.
- Once you feel ready, begin to move slowly and let the eyes softly open, and bring your kindness into the world around you.

NOTES

1 Acharya Buddharakkhita, trans., "Maggavagga: The Path," Dhp 20, *Access to Insight*, http://www.accesstoinsight.org/tipitaka/kn/dhp/dhp.20.budd.html.

2 Eleanor Miles et al., "Does Self-Control Improve with Practice? Evidence from a Six-Week Training Program," *Journal of Experimental Psychology: General* 145, no. 8 (2016): 1075–91, https://doi.org/10.1037/xge0000185.

3 Wilhelm Hofmann et al. "Everyday Temptations: An Experience Sampling Study of Desire, Conflict, and Self-Control," *Journal of Personality and Social Psychology* 102, no. 6 (2012): 1318–35, https://doi.org/10.1037/a0026545.

4 I think it's worth pointing out that for children whose adult role models do not keep their word, eating the first marshmallow can be a wise strategy. Who knows if the promised bonus treat even exists?

5 In the interests of complete openness, those students have a better record than I have. I missed a day three years ago and another last year. My record isn't perfect, but it's still pretty good.

6 Acharya Buddharakkhita, trans., "Papavagga: Evil," Dhp 9, *Access to Insight*, http://www.accesstoinsight.org/tipitaka/kn/dhp/dhp.09.budd.html. Language changed to be gender neutral.

7 This strategy was suggested on the first ever Get Your Sit Together course by one of my meditation students, Brendan Lawler. Thank you, Brendan! Also, I wish my language-learning app could take this approach to a day; I've been caught out more than once by the tyranny of the midnight cutoff.

8 Bhikkhu Bodhi, trans., "The Greater Discourse on the Simile of the Elephant's Footprint," MN 23, https://suttacentral.net/mn28/en/bodhi.

9 Bhikkhu Sujato, trans., "With Asibandhaka's Son," SN 42.6, https://suttacentral.net/sn42.6/en/sujato.

10 Bhikkhu Sujato, trans., "With Bhūmika," MN 126, https://suttacentral.net/mn126/en/sujato.

11 Scholars of the Pali language vigorously debate whether *bodhi* should be translated as "enlightenment" or "awakening." There's support for both views. I like both words, so I use both. When I choose one or the other, it's not to suggest there's some difference between them. It's just that I felt like it.

12 Sniehotta et al., "Action Plans and Coping Plans for Physical Exercise: A Longitudinal Intervention Study in Cardiac Rehabilitation," *British Journal of Health Psychology* 11 (2006). https://pubmed.ncbi.nlm.nih.gov/16480553/.

13 Bhikkhu Anālayo, *Satipaṭṭhāna: The Direct Path to Realization* (Windhorse Publications, 2004), 42.

14 Anālayo, *Satipaṭṭhāna*, 42.

15 Bhikkhu Sujato, trans., "Mindful," SN 47.35, https://suttacentral.net/sn47.35/en/sujato

16 Timothy D. Wilson et al., "Just Think: The Challenges of the Disengaged Mind," *Science* 345, no. 6192 (July 4, 2014): 75–77, https://www.science.org/doi/10.1126/science.1250830.

17 Dvedhāvitakka Sutta, MN 19.

18 Amy Cuddy, "Your body language may shape who you are," https://www.ted.com/talks/amy_cuddy_your_body_language_may_shape_who_you_are.

19 James H. Fowler and Nicholas A. Christakis, "Dynamic Spread of Happiness in a Large Social Network: Longitudinal Analysis over 20 Years in the Framingham Heart Study," *BMJ* 337 (2008):a2338, doi:10.1136/bmj.a2338.

20 Adapted from Bhikkhu Sujato, trans., "The Great Discourse on the Buddha's Extinguishment," DN 16, https://suttacentral.net/dn16/en/sujato.

21 Bhikkhu Sujato, trans., "Sabbath," AN 3.70, https://suttacentral.net/an3.70/en/sujato.

22 Bhikkhu Sujato, trans., AN 2.119, https://suttacentral.net/an2.119/en/sujato.

23 Bhikkhu Sujato, trans., "A Jackal (2nd)," SN 20.12, https://suttacentral.net/sn20.12/en/sujato.

24 Bhikkhu Sujato, trans., "The Longer Discourse with Saccaka," MN 36, https://suttacentral.net/mn36/en/sujato.

25 See Bhikkhu Sujato, trans., "The Great Forty," MN 117, https://suttacentral.net/mn117/en/sujato.

26 Julia C. Basso et al., "Brief, daily meditation enhances attention, memory, mood, and emotional regulation in non-experienced meditators," *Behavioural Brain Research* 356 (2019): 208–20, https://www.sciencedirect.com/science/article/abs/pii/S016643281830322X.

27 University of Waterloo, "Just 10 minutes of meditation helps anxious people have better focus," *ScienceDaily*, https://www.sciencedaily.com/releases/2017/05/170501094325.htm.

28 Michele Solis, "Strategies for Sticking to Your Goals," *Scientific American Mind* 26, no. 1 (January 2015): 7.

29 Bhikkhu Sujato, trans., "Diligence," Dhp 21, https://suttacentral.net/dhp21-32/en/sujato.

30 Thanissaro Bhikkhu, trans., "Appamada Sutta: Heedfulness," AN 10.15, https://www.accesstoinsight.org/tipitaka/an/an10/an10.015.than.html.

31 Bhikkhu Sujato, trans., "Nandiya the Sakyan," SN 55.40, https://suttacentral.net/sn55.40/en/sujato.

32 Carol S. Dweck, *Mindset: The New Psychology of Success* (Ballantine Books, 2006).

33 Bhikkhu Sujato, trans., "Gārava Sutta," SN 6.2. https://suttacentral.net/sn6.2/en/sujato.

34 Bhikkhu Sujato, trans., "Maṅgala Sutta," Snp 2.4. https://suttacentral.net/snp2.4/en/sujato

35 Just about everyone reverses these so that praise is first, putting all the desirable qualities in the left-hand column. However this is the order in which the terms are found in the early scriptures, and I prefer to honor the original source rather than switch things around.

36 Bhikkhu Sujato, trans., "Exterior and Cause Are Not-Self," SN 35.145, https://suttacentral.net/sn35.145/en/sujato.

37 Pema Chödrön, *No Time to Lose: A Timely Guide to the Way of the Bodhisattva* (Shambhala Publications, 2007).

38 *Koans* are brief stories or anecdotes from the Zen tradition that students focus on in order to break down the barriers to enlightenment and provoke sudden spiritual awakening.

39 Bhikkhu Sujato, trans., "A Leash," SN 22.99, https://suttacentral.net/sn22.99/en/sujato.

40 Hilarion Alfeyev, *The Spiritual World of Isaac the Syrian* (Cistercian Publications, 2000), 122.

41 "Advice to Rāhula at Ambalaṭṭhika," MN 31.

42 Thanissaro Bhikkhu, trans., "The Arrow" SN 36.6, https://www.accesstoinsight.org/tipitaka/sn/sn36/sn36.006.than.html. The Pali word is *saññutta*, which is literally "yoked together." Bhikkhu Sujato's translation is "they feel it attached."

43 Fadel Zeidan et al., "Mindfulness Meditation-Based Pain Relief Employs Different Neural Mechanisms Than Placebo and Sham Mindfulness Meditation-Induced Analgesia," *Journal of Neuroscience* 35, no. 46 (November 2015): 15307–15325, https://doi.org/10.1523/JNEUROSCI.2542-15.2015.

44 Gabriel Riegner et al, "Disentangling self from pain: mindfulness meditation–induced pain relief is driven by thalamic-default mode network decoupling," *Pain* 164, no. 2 (February 2023): 280–91, https://pubmed.ncbi.nlm.nih.gov/36095039.

45 Bhikkhu Bodhi, trans., "The Adze Handle," SN 22.101, https://suttacentral.net/sn22.101/en/bodhi.

46 Thanissaro Bhikkhu, trans., "With Cunda," AN 6.46, https://accesstoinsight.org/tipitaka/an/an06/an06.046.than.html.

47 Dhammapada, verse 80, translated by the author.

48 Some translators tell us that satipatthana doesn't mean "foundation" of mindfulness, but something more active: the "establishing" mindfulness. So the four satipatthanas are four areas of our experience in which we establish mindful awareness: the

body, feelings, mind, and the way the processes (*dhammas*) within those can cause or free us from suffering.

49 This exercise is adapted from Stephen R Covey, *The Seven Habits of Highly Effective People* (Simon and Schuster, 1989).

50 "Subjects for Regular Reviewing," AN 5.57.

51 Bhikkhu Sujato, trans., AN 2.19, https://suttacentral.net/an2.19/en/sujato.

52 Bhikkhu Sujato, trans., "With Sāriputta (2nd)," SN 55.5, https://suttacentral.net/sn55.5/en/sujato.

53 Excerpts adapted from *Puja: The Triratna Book of Buddhist Devotional Chants* (Windhorse Publications, 2008).

54 *Shanti* is a Sanskrit word meaning "peace." Chanted three times, it refers to peace in our bodily actions, peace in our communication, and peace within the mind.

INDEX

M

N

ABOUT THE AUTHOR

Bodhipaksa is a Buddhist teacher and author who is originally from Scotland but now lives in New Hampshire. He has practiced in the Triratna Buddhist Community since 1982, and became a member of the Triratna Buddhist Order in 1993. The author of several books, Bodhipaksa also runs Wildmind (http://www.wildmind.org), an online meditation center with a mission to spread compassion and mindfulness through the practice of Buddhist meditation. Most of his teaching is done through Wildmind. Bodhipaksa is the father of two adopted children, and counts his children among his spiritual teachers.

WHAT TO READ NEXT FROM WISDOM PUBLICATIONS

Beyond Distraction
Five Practical Ways to Focus the Mind
Shaila Catherine

"This book contains a wealth of pragmatic advice for both new and experienced meditators, and it will be an invaluable guide for all those journeying on the path to greater freedom."—Joseph Goldstein, author of *Mindfulness: A Practical Guide to Awakening*

Hardcore Zen
Punk Rock, Monster Movies, and the Truth About Reality
Brad Warner

"*Hardcore Zen* is to Buddhism what the Ramones were to rock and roll: A clear-cut, no-bulls**t offering of truth."—Miguel Chen, Teenage Bottlerocket

Daily Wisdom
365 Buddhist Inspirations
Josh Bartok

"One of the basic practices of Buddhism is to remain mindful, and one way this is achieved is simply through reminders. Ranging in length from a sentence to a short page, these reminders include poetry, meditation instruction, practical advice, and thoughts on the way things are."—Brian Bruya, religion editor, Amazon.com

Wholehearted

Slow Down, Help Out, Wake Up

Koshin Paley Ellison

"Intimacy is based on the willingness to open ourselves to many others, to family, friends, and even strangers, forming genuine and deep bonds based on common humanity. Koshin Paley Ellison's teachings share the way forward into a path of connection, compassion, and intimacy."—His Holiness the Dalai Lama

How to Meditate

A Practical Guide

Kathleen McDonald

"Jewels of wisdom and practical experience to inspire you."—Richard Gere

Mindfulness in Plain English

20th Anniversary Edition

Bhante Gunaratana

"A classic—one of the very best English sources for authoritative explanations of mindfulness."—Daniel Goleman, author of *Emotional Intelligence*

Your Life IS Meditation

Mark Van Buren

"You can feel Mark's experiential wisdom coming through each page and into your own practice—or, rather, your entire life. I really love this book!"—Jaimal Yogis, author of *Saltwater Buddha* and *All Our Waves Are Water*

About Wisdom Publications

Wisdom Publications is the leading publisher of classic and contemporary Buddhist books and practical works on mindfulness. To learn more about us or to explore our other books, please visit our website at wisdom.org or contact us at the address below.

Wisdom Publications
132 Perry Street
New York, NY 10014 USA

We are a 501(c)(3) organization, and donations in support of our mission are tax deductible.

Wisdom Publications is affiliated with the Foundation for the Preservation of the Mahayana Tradition (FPMT).